Protecting
the
American
Homeland

Protecting *the* American Homeland

A Preliminary Analysis

Michael E. O'Hanlon   Peter R. Orszag

Ivo H. Daalder   I. M. Destler

David L. Gunter   Robert E. Litan

James B. Steinberg

BROOKINGS INSTITUTION PRESS
Washington, D.C.

Copyright © 2002
THE BROOKINGS INSTITUTION
1775 Massachusetts Avenue, N.W., Washington, D.C. 20036
www.brookings.edu

Library of Congress Cataloging-in-Publication data available.

ISBN 0-8157-0651-0

9 8 7 6 5 4 3 2 1

The paper used in this publication meets minimum requirements of the
American National Standard for Information Sciences—Permanence of Paper for
Printed Library Materials: ANSI Z39.48-1992.

Typeset in Minion

Composition by Cynthia Stock
Silver Spring, Maryland

Printed by R. R. Donnelley and Sons
Harrisonburg, Virginia

CONTENTS

TABLES

FIGURES

PREFACE

Since September 11, there has been no higher priority for the United States than improving its homeland security so that tragic attacks like those experienced on that day might never occur again. Accordingly, the Brookings Institution assembled a multidisciplinary team of scholars to study the problem, assess progress to date, and propose a broad framework for understanding the challenge of homeland security as well as specific steps that the country should now take. While commending the Bush administration, Congress, and many federal, state, local, and private-sector agencies and individuals for their efforts to date, the authors argue for a broader and clearer strategy and offer a proposal for what such a strategy might entail.

The authors would like to extend their gratitude to a number of individuals who helped in the rapid production of this book in important ways. In the Brookings Foreign Policy Studies program, Ellen McHugh, Aaron Moburg-Jones, and Roy Nash made key contributions, as did Jennifer Derstine and Sandip Sukhtankar in the Economic Studies program, and Janet Walker, Tanjam Jacobson, Lawrence Converse, Susan Woollen, and Becky Clark at the Brookings Institution Press. The authors are especially grateful as well to Richard Betts, Ashton Carter, Peter Diamond, Amy Finkelstein, Margaret Hamburg, Howard Kunreuther, Randall Lutter, and Philip Zelikow for comments on earlier drafts, and to Henry Aaron, Robert Cumby, William Dickens, William Gale, Richard Garwin, Michael Janus, and William Perry for useful discussions and help with information on several specific issues. Of course, these individuals bear no responsibility for any mistakes or for the views advanced in the book.

While the authors share collective responsibility for the work, chapters 2 through 5 were drafted by Michael O'Hanlon, Peter Orszag, David Gunter, and James Steinberg; chapter 6 was drafted by Peter Orszag and Robert Litan; and chapter 7 was drafted by Ivo Daalder and Mac Destler.

Protecting
the
American
Homeland

1

INTRODUCTION

The tragic events of September 11 took more than 3,000 lives, caused about $100 billion in direct and indirect economic losses, plunged the United States and many allies and coalition partners into war, and produced substantial increases in security spending.[1] That date is already among the most important in the nation's history, and its policy implications will reverberate for many years, if not decades. In this book, we ask how vulnerable the United States is to further terrorist attacks and what can realistically be done to protect the nation without unduly impeding its economic prosperity or way of life.

The debate on these issues has advanced significantly since September 11. More important, thanks to the efforts of many Americans at home and abroad, the country has become considerably more secure against terrorist attack. Even so, significant vulnerabilities to terrorist attack remain.

To be sure, a large, free, and open country cannot make itself invulnerable to terrorism. Nonetheless, an effective homeland security strategy can substantially complicate the efforts of any terrorist group attempting to strike at the country, thereby making the most deadly and costly types of terrorist attack less likely to succeed. Hence good homeland security is far from hopeless, though efforts to date have not been sufficient.

The Bush administration's budget plan for fiscal year 2003, unveiled in February 2002, includes $38 billion in proposed federal homeland security spending. This budget would build on accomplishments to date and make the country more secure. However, it has two significant shortcomings, perhaps reflecting the short period of time that the administration has had to develop its proposals, as well as the large number of disparate individuals, agencies, and members of Congress who effectively shared responsibility for its creation. First, the budget focuses more on preventing recurrences of attacks like those in 2001—through airliners or anthrax—than on reducing vulnerability in our society more comprehensively. It thus concentrates on the "last war" rather than the possible next one. Second, it emphasizes protecting targets within the United States against attacks rather than taking domestic steps to prevent those attacks in the first place (for example, by tracking potential terrorists and preventing access to dangerous materials). The difficulty with focusing primarily on protecting targets within the United States is that there is a large number of attractive targets and a wide array of methods of attack. Even if significant resources are dedicated to protect some sites, terrorists can shift their efforts toward less-protected ones (the problem of "displacement"). Preventive activities, on the other hand, tend to reduce the overall level of risk without having to know in advance what the targets are, while also complementing the site defenses. Key to any successful prevention against future attacks will be the effective use of information technology (for the collection, sharing, and deployment of key data), as well as substantial increases in staffing for the government agencies responsible for border enforcement and domestic antiterrorism activities.

Prevention is not a panacea; no matter how well we refine our strategies, we will not succeed in identifying all dangerous people and keeping all lethal materials away from terrorists. We must also work to minimize the consequences of an attack, including through prompt and effective response mechanisms. A successful strategy must therefore combine prevention, protection, and consequences management, as our proposals recommend.

The administration itself recognizes that its current plan is incomplete. Governor Tom Ridge and his Office of Homeland Security continue to work on a strategic plan for protecting the United States that would tie together the now rather disjointed set of individual initiatives and would presumably include a number of new initiatives not yet contained in the $38 billion budget request.

The purpose of this study is to provide a framework for thinking about how to address the country's vulnerabilities and to identify key priorities and approaches to eliminate or reduce those vulnerabilities. It also suggests an approach to identifying who should pay for which counterterrorism measures, and proposes ways the government could be more effectively organized to carry out its new set of critical national security tasks.

Broadening and Reorienting the Homeland Security Agenda

The basic thrust of the Bush administration's plan is to prevent recurrences of tragedies similar to those of September 11, as well as the subsequent anthrax attacks, by improving airport and airline security, beginning to link the databases of various law enforcement and intelligence agencies so that information on suspects can be widely shared and promptly used, stockpiling vaccines and antibiotics against biological attack, researching better antidotes to biological attack, improving the public health infrastructure needed to detect biological attacks and treat their victims, better equipping and training local responders for any mass-casualty attack, and making modest improvements in border security. Although many specifics merit scrutiny, these basic priorities are sound, and the funding requested for addressing most of them appears roughly appropriate. But there remain significant unmet needs, and these specific initiatives must be brought within a more comprehensive strategy.

To broaden and reorient the homeland security agenda, we propose a four-tier strategic framework consisting of (1) perimeter security at the country's borders, (2) preventive activities within the country, (3) protection of domestic sites, and (4) consequence management after attacks.[2] The Bush administration's 2003 budget contains initiatives that are broadly similar to what we believe is required in the first and final categories but does not provide an appropriate plan for the other two: domestic prevention and protection. We develop a more systematic and comprehensive agenda in those areas.

By our estimates, even if the entire $38 billion Bush homeland security budget were implemented, a further $5 billion to $10 billion a year in federal funds could be spent effectively beyond the Bush budget to adopt additional measures that promise considerable security benefits for a modest cost. (See chapter 8 and appendix B for a detailed description of the Bush homeland security budget.) Specifically, we recommend the following measures:

—Major improvements and expansions in the Coast Guard and Customs Service, well beyond those already suggested by the Bush administration.

—Substantial expansions in domestic law enforcement agencies (again, well beyond those proposed by the Bush administration) and in the linking together and modernization of their databases.

—Various measures for reducing the odds that biological agents could circulate through the air intake systems of major buildings and other large facilities.

—Changes in the nation's food safety programs.

—Additional measures for protecting buildings against conventional explosives and fires.

—Improved security measures for the nation's nuclear power plants, toxic chemical plants, and biological research facilities.

—A new approach to monitoring and protecting the nation's airspace.

—More background checks for drivers of trucks carrying hazardous materials and other related safety measures.

—Numerous specific protective measures for other types of public and private infrastructure.

For each initiative, we provide a very rough estimate of the likely costs. We also include a detailed analysis of who should pay for these various measures and how the federal government should be organized to ensure their effective implementation.

A Framework for Protecting the Homeland

In theory, one could organize a homeland security strategy by trying to identify specific threats to the United States, with responses to each. This "threat-based" approach would attempt to identify the full range of potential terrorists and to discern their intentions and strategies. While such an analysis might prove a useful supplement to the approach we propose here, the difficulties of identifying the full range of potential malefactors, and their ability to adjust their strategies and targets opportunistically (rather than pursue a consistent modus operandi), suggest that we will be unlikely to predict with high confidence when or where they will attack.

Hence our strategy focuses on preventing attacks that would pose the greatest harm to our national interests—as measured by the lives of citizens, our economy, the functioning of key institutions, and our way of life. Any homeland security strategy must be complemented by a vigorous policy to preempt terrorists abroad, by military, diplomatic, financial, law enforcement, and other means, but those efforts are outside the scope of this study. The most effective way to avoid attacks that would cause serious harm to our homeland would be to identify and thwart the perpetrators from reaching the United States, and from bringing with them the means of destruction, in the first place. That is why the first tier of our strategy focuses on securing our perimeter. This means keeping out dangerous people and dangerous objects—notably, weapons of mass destruction, threatening aircraft and cruise missiles, high explosives, antiaircraft missiles such as the Stinger, and certain other weapons—before attacks can be planned and launched. Because no perimeter strategy can ever be foolproof, and because some attacks may come from individuals within the United States using dangerous materials available domestically, the second tier of our strategy is domestic prevention—identifying would-be terrorists in the United States and securing dangerous materials so that they cannot be misappropriated by terrorists. Since both forms of prevention will inevitably be imperfect, the third task is protection of key potential targets. This is a particularly daunting policy challenge, since there is a virtually unlimited number of targets. We therefore need a framework to prioritize our effort at protection.

To implement this approach we have developed a rough rank ordering of attacks we wish to prevent or mitigate—based on key variables of national interest (number of casualties, extent of economic damage, harm to key institutions and sites of high symbolic significance). Although there are inevitably issues of comparability (is a modest loss of lives more serious than a major hit against our economy?), we believe it is possible to develop a rough "ordinal" ranking of vulnerabilities that can guide policymakers in prioritizing our goals and our expenditures.

It is impossible to specify analytically how much risk we as a society should be prepared to run, and how much security is "enough"—that is a political decision, to be made by the political process. But this approach should lead to a cost-effective homeland security agenda, so that each additional dollar of spending is directed to achieving the greatest benefit in lives saved, costs averted, and so forth.

Tables 1-1 through 1-3 illustrate this general approach. Table 1-1 ranks attacks by the level of potential casualties. Table 1-2 shows the potential impact of different kinds of attacks on the economy. Table 1-3 gives a rough estimate of the key institutions and symbolic sites whose destruction would not only entail casualties and economic losses, but also have high intangible value. Some attacks will rank high on all three scales—the World Trade Center attack is a clear example. Others may largely figure in just one or another.

The specific areas of major American vulnerability could even change over time.[3] That is why a key component of any homeland security agenda should be to create a "red team" within the U.S. government that would

Table 1-1. *Possible Scale of Terrorist Attacks*

Type of atack	Possible fatalities	Estimated likelihood
Efficient biological attack (for example, clandestine wide dispersal of a contagious agent such as ebola, smallpox, or anthrax)	1,000,000	Extremely low
Atomic bomb detonated in major U.S. city	100,000	Very low
Successful attack on nuclear or toxic chemical plant	10,000	Very low
Simple, relatively inefficient biological or chemical attack in one skyscraper or stadium	1,000	Low
Conventional attack on a single train, airplane	250–500	Low
Suicide attack with explosives or firearms in a mall or crowded street	50–100	Modest

Source: Office of Technology Assessment, *Proliferation of Weapons of Mass Destruction: Assessing the Risks* (U.S. Congress, 1993).

Table 1-2. *Economic Disruption as a Result of Terrorism*

Nature of attack	Nature of economic disruption	Potential costs
Weapons of mass destruction shipped via containers, mail	Extended shutdown in deliveries; physical destruction and lost production in contaminated area; massive loss of life; medical treatment for survivors	Up to $1 trillion
Efficient release of biological agent through much of a major urban area	Disruption to economic activity in affected area; threat to confidence and economic operations in other areas; massive loss of life; medical expenses	$750 billion
Widespread terror against key elements of public economy across nation (malls, restaurants, movie theaters, etc.)	Significant and sustained decline in economic activity in public spaces; associated drop in consumer confidence	$250 billion
Attack on interstate natural gas pipelines in Southeast United States	Natural gas shortages in Northeast and Midwest; significant reduction in economic activity in Northeast; loss of life from direct attacks and from heat/cold; destruction of physical capital	$150 billion
Large attacks that expose a finite and reparable vulnerability (like 9/11)	Substantial but temporary weakening of economy due to direct (loss of human life and physical capital) and indirect effects (decline in confidence and network failures)	$100 billion
Cyberattack on computer systems regulating regional electric power, combined with physical attacks on transmission and distribution network	Regional electricity shortages that persist for a week; health risks from heat/cold; interruption of production schedules; destruction of physical capital	$25 billion
Bombings or bomb scares	Effective shutting down of several major cities for a day	$10 billion

Note: The attacks postulated in this table, and even their relative rankings, are illustrative and speculative. In addition to other economic costs, the estimates above assume an economic value for human life in the range proposed in Richard Layard and Stephen Glaister, *Cost-Benefit Analysis* (Cambridge University Press, 1994).

Table 1-3. *Estimated Political Costs of Attacks against U.S. Icons,*
Assuming Few if Any Casualties

Type of target	Examples of specific targets	Hypothesized effects
Core national structures	White House, Capitol, Supreme Court	Greater confidence for terrorists, less confidence for U.S. citizens, impression of government weakness at home and abroad, inability to protect core political institutions, enormous global publicity, greater U.S. resolve to act
Other key U.S. monuments, assets	Statue of Liberty, Washington Monument, Lincoln Memorial, Mount Rushmore, Liberty Bell	Similar to above but possibly fewer implications for image of government
Other important political structures	Pentagon, state capitols, State Department, Treasury building, FBI building, foreign embassies and consulates in the U.S.	Similar to first category but slightly less important, though hard to quantify
Other icons	Cape Canaveral, St. Louis Gate to West, Empire State Building, Sears Tower, Space Needle, presidential libraries, cathedrals, and so on	Limited impact on domestic and global impressions about U.S. and its ability to defend itself, moderate global publicity

identify vulnerabilities as they evolve and design mock attacks to exploit them. Many of its efforts would be classified, though some public debate would be needed to formulate budget allocations or other significant policy decisions to address the risks.[4]

One consequence of this strategy may be to displace the potential targets of terrorists from attacks with large consequences to those with lesser ones. On the margin, this is clearly preferable, but it also illustrates why prevention must be the highest priority (since it stops all attacks, large and small), and why the list of vulnerabilities must be continuously reviewed, so that the displacement effect does not uncover heretofore unthought-of targets with large consequences.[5]

None of this is to deny that even a number of small attacks might have a broad impact on our way of life, creating fear disproportionate to the level of exposure. But since resources are finite, and there are costs associated with both protection and prevention (financial, civil liberties, and so on), we believe this approach is the soundest strategy and will substantially reduce the odds of extremely costly and harmful terrorist attacks.

Finally, since even a well-designed strategy of prevention and protection will not always be successful, the fourth task is to manage the consequences of any attacks that still may occur, or to reduce their toll and their indirect consequences.

As chapters 2–5 explain in more detail, our proposals would expand annual federal spending on homeland security to about $45 billion, or some $25 billion above the amount originally planned for 2002 and more than $10 billion above final 2002 levels. (These costs include many homeland security expenditures within the Department of Defense but not efforts to defeat terrorism overseas, such as intelligence or military operations in Afghanistan, or missile defense.)[6] Up to another $10 billion would be borne by the private sector. The federal government's resulting homeland security budget would represent an increase of between $5 billion and $10 billion above the Bush administration's proposed 2003 budget for homeland security. The total federal budget costs, while substantial, would represent no more than 0.5 percent of GDP, in contrast to military spending of more than 3 percent of GDP. To finance this expansion without causing a further deterioration in the nation's longer-term fiscal outlook, we support freezing at least part of the tax cuts passed as part of the Economic Growth and Tax Relief and Reconciliation Act of 2001 that have not yet taken effect.[7]

The Role of Government in Homeland Security

Another critical issue is who should implement and pay for the various new security measures? For perimeter security, identification of terrorists within the United States, and consequence mitigation, it seems apparent that this will largely be a government function, although the locus of government responsibility will vary. For protection of dangerous materials and targets, the answer is less obvious. In chapter 6 we argue that there is a role for government in protecting against terrorist attacks on private property within the United States, since such attacks often have societal and national security implications that transcend the immediate private damage they cause. But the government should not always foot the bill. In many private sector settings, the various users, providers, and owners of the property or activity should pay for at least some of the antiterrorism costs. In other words, those who benefit most directly from a given property or activity should pay to protect it as a general rule.

In most cases, government intervention should take the form of mandates on the private sector rather than through direct subsidies or tax incentives. Over the longer term, the most auspicious approach involves regulation coupled with requirements or incentives for terrorism insurance. The mandates should be set at relatively low levels at first, especially given the uncertainties involved and the high costs that could result, for example, from retrofitting existing buildings and other property to meet very high safety standards.

Furthermore, to reduce the costs involved and provide incentives for additional, cost-effective security measures, the government should offer an "EZ-pass" approach whenever possible. That is, individuals or firms willing to undergo additional security background checks or willing to undertake additional security measures should receive some benefit in exchange, for example, in the form of expedited clearance through Immigration or Customs or lower insurance premiums.

Within the public sector, the federal government should finance those steps that specifically and primarily address terrorist threats. But state and local governments should finance those antiterrorism measures that provide substantial benefits to their own jurisdictions (in addition to affecting their ability to prevent or address terrorist attacks). The larger the local benefit of a specific antiterrorism measure, the larger the local and state share of the costs should be. For example, the federal government should finance specialized antiterrorism training and equipment for police and fire departments but should not finance the hiring of additional police or firefighters.[8]

Organizing the Homeland Security Effort

In chapter 7, we examine how to structure the government to address homeland security issues. Most proposals today seek to consolidate widely dispersed authorities and agencies into one or more new, central structures. Although some consolidation may make sense—particularly of agencies responsible for securing the nation's borders—centralization cannot be the main answer to this formidable challenge. The responsibility for preparing for, preventing, and, if necessary, responding to a terrorist incident is widely dispersed across the executive branch; it is also shared by state and local authorities. The private sector has a critical role to play as well. By its very nature, homeland security is a highly decentralized activity, with widely dispersed functions that simply cannot be brought under a single roof. What is needed instead is leadership, coordination, and mobilization of the responsible agencies and their leaders, at the federal, state, and local levels. That is precisely the task President Bush has handed Governor Ridge. Given the number of agencies, interests, and people involved, it is a task of truly mammoth proportions. But the job is doable, and past experiences in parallel coordinating efforts—for national security and economic policy—provide valuable lessons on how to go about the task.

Within such a coordinating context, some consolidation of functionally similar activities (such as dealing with border security, law enforcement, and Defense Department activities in support of civilian efforts) makes sense, as would enhancing Ridge's authority over budgetary matters and making his position subject to Senate confirmation. But on their own, the structural reforms championed by many critics of the current arrangement will be of little help and could well undercut Ridge's ability to influence the broad range of government activity, which he can never control directly in any event.

2

SECURING AMERICA'S PERIMETER

Apart from offensive uses of military and intelligence assets overseas to thwart terrorists before they even approach U.S. shores, perimeter defense offers the first line of homeland security against a terrorist attack. It is intended to prevent terrorists and threatening objects from gaining access to the nation, whether by air, sea, road, or rail, or on foot.[1] Table 2-1 lists the major areas of potential defensive activity, and table 2-2 presents our specific suggested policy steps in each.

Many of these steps could incur substantial economic costs, since they would increase waiting times for people (and goods) at the borders and therefore interfere with international trade and the flow of workers.[2] Some could be implemented with low or moderate cost to the federal government and without damaging the normal workings of the national economy or seriously inconveniencing Americans. By way of example, improved visa and passport procedures could produce tighter security at relatively low cost without substantial increases—and potentially even a reduction—in waiting times for most travelers. Measures of intermediate cost that would impose a limited burden on the economy would be to inspect most cargo during loading overseas. And a

Table 2-1. *Perimeter Defense*

Area of defense	Activity
Air	Air defense
	Cruise and ballistic missile defense systems
	Airport security
Sea	Coast protection
	Cargo security
	Seaport security
Road and rail	Ports of entry security
	Unmanned border monitoring
People	Visa processing
	Document integrity enhancements
	Document checks

high-cost effort might be to inspect most cargo at home using traditional techniques and a massively expanded Customs Service. The various examples developed in this chapter are grouped by their rough costs (table 2-2) and their likely effects on reducing U.S. vulnerabilities. Note that table 2-2 includes national ballistic missile defense, but a discussion of such options is beyond the scope of this study, apart from the related issues of air defense and cruise missile defense.[3] The Bush administration similarly excludes national missile defense from its homeland security budget.

Throughout the volume, the cost estimates for our proposals should be viewed as ballpark rather than precise figures. Some derive from specific homeland security programs that have been designed in detail, but many others are based on analogy with programs of roughly comparable difficulty and cost in other government sectors. If the Bush administration has offered a related, major initiative in its 2003 budget request, the initiative is designated by a footnote.

Air

To minimize terrorist attacks by air, the United States should consider improvements to its air defense and cruise missile defense. (It also needs to

Table 2-2. *Proposals to Improve U.S. Perimeter Defense against Terrorism*

Area of defense	Specific measure	Approximate annual cost[a] (billions of dollars)
Preferred options		
Air	Runway-alert perimeter air defense	1.0
	Research and development program for national cruise missile defense[b]	1.0[c]
Sea	Improved port security planning, procedures, personnel[b]	1.0
	Expansion of U.S. Coast Guard	1.8
	Expansion of Customs capabilities[b]	2.5
Road and rail	Expanded INS staffing outside Border Patrol[b]	0.3
	Expanded border patrols[b]	0.3
People	Linking of INS, FBI, Customs, CIA databases	0.3
	Bolstered State Department visa review processes and personnel	0.3
	Total	8.3
Other higher-cost/ least-risk options		
Air	Cruise missile defense	2.0
	Expanded continuous air patrols over more major cities	1.5 above current costs
Road and rail, air, sea	Comprehensive customs procedures in the United States	At least 10.0

a. Annual cost relative to original pre-9/11 2002 budget. Here and elsewhere, investment costs are amortized over a ten-year period.

b. Denotes similar initiative of comparable magnitude proposed by the Bush administration.

c. Above existing program.

improve airport security systems. But since expanded security at airports affects domestic flights as well as international flights, we address airport security in chapter 4 on internal security.)

Broaden Air Defense

After September 11, the U.S. Air Force—principally its reserve components—flew about 2,500 sorties a month over the United States.[4] The administration has requested $1.3 billion for such efforts in 2003, roughly the same rate of spending, about $100 million a month, since September 11, though it is reviewing other options for airspace security as well, and reducing air patrols gradually as it does so. In fact, it may be better to make air defense more systematic and comprehensive nationwide, but reduce the number of air patrols since they can protect only a small number of cities against a type of attack that has now become rather unlikely in any event.[5]

These continuous combat air patrols have put a significant strain on U.S. air defense systems because at present the military maintains just four squadrons of dedicated air defense interceptor aircraft, or a total of about 75 serviceable planes. Of course, it also bases roughly 25 wings of aircraft—some 2,000 planes in all—on American territory, counting the U.S.-based elements of its 20 Air Force fighter wings, 11 Navy carrier wings, and 3 Marine Corps wings. These aircraft can provide a relatively good screen for the country's perimeters, with fighter combat bases of one type or another in various states.[6] Most of the time, aircraft are not on call for immediate response, but they can be made quickly available. After September 11, combat aircraft operating from 26 bases provided air patrols over 15 key areas of the country, sometimes continuously and sometimes by keeping planes on 15-minute runway alert.[7] (These patrols have subsequently been curtailed but continue over at least Washington, D.C.)

After September 11, about 30,000 Air Force National Guard and Reserve personnel were called up (out of a total of 175,000), with about 11,000 operating from some of the above locations to provide enhanced security for domestic airspace.[8] North Atlantic Treaty Organization (NATO) forces from other countries also provided hundreds of troops to man and maintain five NATO AWACS aircraft. The Army called up just under 20,000 reservists (out of 550,000 in the Army National Guard and Reserves combined); this is not a particularly large burden, and about 6,000 of those called up are helping to provide airport security in a manner that may prove only temporary until airport security forces can be manned. The Navy—which provided most of the personnel in the vicinity of South Asia during the autumn of 2001—called up just under 10,000 (out of 90,000); about 1,500 Marine reservists (out of 40,000) served as well. Therefore it is the Air Force that faces the greatest dilemma in any effort to sustain vigorous homeland security well into the future. Since it cannot keep one-sixth of its reserve component on active duty indefinitely, there is a good case for adding active-duty forces to a continental air defense system or for changing how the mission is conducted.

As for surveillance of airspace, the United States generally has at least two dozen of its AWACS aircraft available at any time. But most are located in Oklahoma, not necessarily a strategic spot for protecting the country's borders and major cities. Strong consideration should be given to relocating some of these aircraft elsewhere.

Is this network good enough? That all depends on how quickly it could recognize a terrorist-controlled airplane. Virtually no practical air defense system could stop a hijacked plane that gave no indication of its intentions before plowing into a major building in a city or that was mistakenly believed to be a flight that was accidentally off course (in a situation in which insufficient time was available to contact the pilots). The current U.S. air defense system would be adequate for intercepting a plane identified hours from U.S. shores. But if such a plane was only recognized once it was, say, half an hour from its target, interceptor aircraft (or air defense missiles) would have to be based nearby. Similarly, where Federal Aviation Administration (FAA) radars are incapable of tracking all approaches to the United States, it might be necessary to augment its coverage of airspace with military assets.

One way to tighten the nation's air defense capabilities for the latter medium-warning situations might be to place a modest number of additional aircraft on alert along certain parts of the country's borders where current coverage is limited, and to have at least two to four aircraft on call at existing fighter bases. What additional demands would this place on the nation's air superiority aircraft? Having aircraft on call at existing fighter bases might require nothing more than asking pilots to be on standby (but presumably at home with their families on off hours) once or twice a month. However, it might be necessary to add simple operating bases at a few sites—Texas, northern California, Maine, perhaps two or three other sites—where existing protection is limited at present. Several aircraft could be deployed from their home bases to these simple operating bases at any time. But to maintain just four aircraft at six more bases continuously, even if they were generally on the ground with engines off, would require perhaps a full wing of 72 aircraft and twice as many pilots (together with associated support crews).

If existing aircraft could be used, only personnel and operating costs might go up substantially, for a total of perhaps $250 million a year. However, it is conceivable that added personnel and equipment might be needed. Suppose that 10,000 personnel were added to the force along with half a wing of aircraft (30,000 reservists were called up in the fall of 2001, but we assume a more efficient type of airspace protection here).[9] In addition, it would be necessary to upgrade communications systems for certain existing aircraft such as F-15s to make them more effective in an air defense mode. The total added cost under this scenario would be about $1 billion a year.[10]

This cost could be added to the administration's request of $1.3 billion for continuous air patrols for 2003. But that $1.3 billion should be rethought. If continuous air patrols are really necessary, they should extend their operations to a dozen or so of the nation's largest cities, most of which have large skyscrapers that could be attacked by aircraft. In that case, continuous air patrols might cost $3 billion or more. But the measures taken to protect aircraft since September 11 may make such patrols unnecessary, even near the nation's largest cities. Thus the runway alert option could actually save money on balance.

Create a Cruise Missile Defense System

Relative to the long-range ballistic missile threat that has so dominated public debates for years, the cruise missile threat is both more plausible and more difficult to defend against. That makes it all the harder to decide whether a dedicated defense system is required here. In any case, no answer should be attempted before the issue is explored.

Cruise missiles are small and relatively easy to hide on ships or other vehicles that could approach U.S. territory before the missile was fired. They are sufficiently small and deployable for some terrorists possibly to acquire.

Reconfiguring a standard cruise missile to carry a primitive nuclear warhead, likely to weigh half a ton or more, is probably beyond their capabilities, but outfitting a cruise missile with a dispensing mechanism for distributing chemical or biological agents might not be. In this sense, the cruise missile threat could pose a risk of serious harm along the three parameters identified in chapter 1 (casualties, economic, high intangible value) and thus it is worth considering serious measures to counter it.

To protect the country against cruise missiles reliably is a very difficult proposition, given the multiplicity of possible launch points, approach trajectories, and targets. But a radar system, perhaps kept airborne by aerostat balloons, together with some surface-to-air missile sites, should be able to provide at least some coverage of the nation's borders. Such a network might not provide leakproof defense in all places, but it should stop small, simple attacks with high confidence. Hence most possible attackers could never be certain that their cruise missiles would reach U.S. territory once fired.[11]

Ideally, a cruise missile defense plan would intervene before missiles were launched (for example, through interception of cruise-missile carrying ships and aircraft). But even the best surveillance would be unlikely to prevent all missile launchings from dozens of miles off American shores. For these reasons, defenses against cruise missiles themselves would be needed too.

To provide such defenses, the United States would have to be able to detect the missiles and then launch nearby interceptors quickly enough to destroy the missiles before they reached targets. Detection could only be accomplished with continuous radar coverage of all approaches to U.S. territory. Here the key variables are the power and range of the radar equipment and the altitude at which it can be situated. Radar on the ground, even on hills, has a limited range owing to the curvature of the earth and the low altitudes at which cruise missiles customarily fly. If cruise missiles could fly as low as 50 feet, say, while radar by necessity was situated mainly near shorelines on hills measuring, say, 100 to 200 feet, radar stations would have to be placed every 15 to 20 miles around the entire perimeter of the United States to give several minutes' warning of attack. By contrast, aircraft or aerostats at altitudes of several thousand feet could be used to provide surveillance and targeting information and thus could be spaced every 100 to 200 miles, reducing the total need to several dozen for the entire country. However, two to four radars could be needed to keep one on continuous station.[12]

The intercept mission is more complicated, since it depends on the distance at which enemy missiles might be launched. Launches by ship or plane within a couple of miles of U.S. territory could overwhelm even a very dense network of shore-based interceptors. Unless interceptors were located within, say, 5 to 10 miles of any such point, they would not be able to reach the incoming cruise missile quickly enough to prevent it from reaching its target.

Two important considerations here are how much warning could be expected under this scenario and how close could the enemy realistically launch its attack? If ships posed the main threat of cruise missile attack, careful Coast Guard monitoring (see the next section) could identify suspicious vessels entering U.S. territorial waters and contiguous zones. Assuming that they could be stopped at the outer edges of the contiguous zone, which extends out to 24 nautical miles—and fired upon immediately if they did not—it should be possible to prevent the launch of cruise missiles from closer than roughly 20 nautical miles, or about 25 standard miles. For a relatively simple subsonic cruise missile, that means interceptors would have about 5 minutes of flight time to do their work before targets on land were struck.

These timelines translate into a difficult, but not impossible, job of protecting coastal regions. If defenses had to be deployed uniformly around American coastlines and interceptor missiles could accelerate quickly and then travel at roughly two-thirds of a mile per second, it might suffice to have a base of several interceptors every 50 miles or so. If the main goal is to protect high-value targets, such as larger towns and cities as well as key ports and infrastructure, however, fewer interceptors would be required along certain stretches of coastline, where they might be spaced every 100 to 200 miles. Either way, given that the length of U.S. coastal zones is several thousand miles, many dozens of interceptor bases would be needed.

All told, a rudimentary cruise missile defense for the United States could probably cost $10 billion to $20 billion (making for perhaps $1 billion to $2 billion a year in annual investment costs, depending on the period over which deployment occurred). It would cost an additional $300 million to $1 billion per year to operate.[13] These figures would represent a modest investment on the scale of national ballistic missile defense, but a large one in relation to most other homeland security requirements.[14]

There is a safety question to consider here, too: a national cruise missile defense system might pose a threat to small aircraft, which at times look a great deal like cruise missiles. A terrorist might even try to turn a manned aircraft into a cruise missile to avoid radar identification. To address this concern, all aircraft could be required to fly with transponders similar to the identification-friend-or-foe (IFF) systems on military aircraft. Even so, some pilots might ignore the requirement for transponders, others might fail to maintain their IFF devices in good working order, and still others might be shot at by mistake despite doing everything right. In other words, even if the nation were prepared to shoulder the budgetary expense of a cruise missile defense, it might not be ready to accept the potential toll in innocent victims. For that reason, the cruise missile defense concept is especially difficult to assess. As a practical matter, it might only work against missiles fired from much further off shore, or in time of crisis, when a suspicious object could quickly be identified as threatening. For this reason, assessing the value of cruise missile defense also requires carefully assessing the risk that cruise missiles might be used by a state adversary as well as by terrorists.

Sea (Cargoes and Port Security)

Another avenue of terrorist attack could be the sea. The Coast Guard, the Customs Service, and local port security represent the three crucial means of bolstering the nation's defense against terrorist access by sea (though the Navy and even the Air Force might help under certain circumstances as well). Although the Bush administration has taken some serious steps in this area, much more needs to be done.

Expand the Coast Guard

The U.S. Coast Guard, which provides the country's principal defense against illicit shipping, would be a major barrier to terrorist attacks in which explosives or weapons of mass destruction were headed for an American city on a ship (see appendix D). The Coast Guard also is responsible for preventing any attacks against U.S. littoral regions, including major ports that would be needed in military contingencies. In addition, the Coast Guard rescues boaters, protects fisheries, ensures environmental protection in America's exclusive economic zones, and prevents drug smuggling, all still important missions in the post–September 11 world.[15]

The Coast Guard performs all these missions on about $6 billion a year (channeled mainly through the Department of Transportation budget). It employs about 35,000 active-duty personnel, making it roughly one-fifth the size of the Marine Corps and less than one-tenth the size of each of the other military services. Furthermore, good, up-to-date equipment is in short supply, and many of its ships are facing block obsolescence. Viewed as a navy, its fleet of larger, deepwater surface vessels would reportedly rank third oldest among the world's 40 main naval powers. Hampered by equipment breakdowns and vessels slower than those operated by most outlaws, the Coast Guard is having increasing difficulty carrying out its duties. Unfortunately, projected budgets will only allow it to replace its larger ships (primarily cutters longer than 100 feet) and airplanes over the next fifty years, as reflected in the Coast Guard's "Deepwater" plan.[16]

To meet priority requirements would require recapitalizing the Coast Guard's large ships and aircraft over a period of no more than 20 years. That would necessitate an annual budget increase of some $300 million.[17] Other initiatives are also needed, as was clear even before September 11. According to a recent task force, the Coast Guard should improve its protective measures against chemical or biological attack, a demand that would drive up annual costs by several tens of millions of dollars or more.[18] The Coast Guard is already trying to modernize its command and control systems through the National Distress and Response System Modernization Project (NDRSMP).

The magnitude of the overall dollar shortfall is underscored by the additional tasks assigned to the Coast Guard since September 11. By December, more than 100 security zones had been established around facilities such as major naval bases, key landmarks like the Statue of Liberty, and oil refineries near major cities.[19] All vessels in New York harbor were inspected; other prominent ports and cities such as New Orleans were heavily guarded; waters near certain of the country's 68 nuclear power plants located along navigable waterways were patrolled; cruise ships were boarded and searched.[20] Sea marshals were placed on certain ships as they approached port to ensure that no harm could be inflicted on people or major infrastructure such as bridges by those ships. All six of the Coast Guard's port security units, which reside primarily in its reserve component, were called up to active duty.[21] This amounted to nearly a tenfold increase in such security measures altogether.

Given that 1,000 foreign-flag ships reach U.S. shores every week, the post–September 11 security environment presents the Coast Guard with an enormous challenge.[22] In the aftermath of the attacks, about 60 percent of deployed Coast Guard assets were devoted to port and waterway security, including about 50 cutters, 40 to 50 aircraft, and hundreds of small boats.[23] Since those assets were also used at a higher than normal rate, port and waterway security alone has equaled the demands normally placed on the full Coast Guard fleet operating at normal tempo. Thirteen Navy ships were made available to help the Coast Guard with its increased mission.[24] Otherwise, the only way to handle these new demands was to sharply curtail other Coast Guard activities, typically to 25 percent or less of their previous levels, and to ask most personnel to work very long hours.[25]

In view of these pressures, how much larger and more expensive should the Coast Guard become? Many of the missions added after September 11 seem likely to remain important indefinitely. But the current pace of operations need not remain as high, according to the Coast Guard's commandant, Admiral James M. Loy.[26] Efficiencies can be found, largely through the work of local port security committees composed of local, state, and federal officials who will devise security plans for individual ports.[27] In the end, homeland security may take no more than 25 percent of total Coast Guard effort.[28] With improved forward screening procedures for ships headed toward U.S. waters, the fleet should be able to make more efficient use of its assets to protect key facilities and rely less on simple brute-force inspection techniques. Keep-out zones might be enforced through a combination of remote sensors, unmanned aerial vehicles, fixed impediments to ship movement, and even shore-based guns as a last resort. Where that is not possible, the Coast Guard may be able to use smaller boats—perhaps with upgraded armaments—in place of larger ships like cutters for such coastal and inland sites. But on the whole, the Coast Guard will need to grow considerably.

How does one translate these various considerations into specific recommendations for an alternative Coast Guard fleet and budget? The Coast

Guard includes five broad classes of assets: large ships (generally known as cutters, designed for use as far as 50 miles from shore or more), smaller boats, special-purpose vessels such as icebreakers and buoytenders, aircraft, and shore facilities.[29] Today's Coast Guard includes roughly 90 of the larger cutters, just over 300 smaller boats, about 90 special-purpose vessels, roughly 200 aircraft, and a wide range of shore-based assets.

For the kind of intensive coastal patrolling that may be needed in the aftermath of September 11, the smaller ships are likely to be most useful, though modest increases in other assets may be desirable as well. The post–September 11 Coast Guard might therefore look roughly as follows: 100 larger cutters, a doubling to 600 smaller ships and boats to handle old and new missions near shore, 90 special-purpose vessels, 200 to 250 aircraft, and essentially the same shore infrastructure as today. (Some boats might be leased in the short term to permit a rapid increase in fleet size.) That means costs would be about double in one of five major Coast Guard expenditure areas, with modest increases elsewhere. Hence the total Coast Guard budget might permanently be in the neighborhood of $7 billion a year.[30]

Bolster Customs Service

The Coast Guard's efforts to provide security along waterways can be aided by the Customs Service, whose chief responsibility is to find and stop illicit cargo, whether on ships, trucks, or aircraft. (Thus this option is relevant for the road and rail network as well as for maritime approaches to the country.) It has a budget of about $2.4 billion, which supports some 20,000 employees monitoring trade at 300 points of entry and at borders elsewhere. Its primary task is to collect tariffs and prevent prohibited products (such as certain foods and illegal drugs—or weapons) from entering the United States.

Post–September 11 changes at Customs should encompass not only its size and capabilities, but also its procedures. Until recently, Customs typically inspected about 2 percent of containers arriving at U.S. shores and less than 5 percent of containers arriving overland from Mexico.[31] These figures may be closer to 10 percent since September 11 owing to strenuous efforts by existing inspectors but even at that remain quite modest.[32] Yet these containers may be the primary means by which a terrorist would sneak many types of weapons into the United States.[33] A much more comprehensive and lasting improvement in inspections procedures is therefore needed.

This is clearly a daunting task. In 2001, about 500 million people, 125 million vehicles, and 21.4 million import shipments entered the United States.[34] Inspecting all of them, instead of the current small percentage, could push Customs' $2.4 billion annual budget well over the $50 billion mark. Even if considerable economies of scale were possible and less than 100 percent of all incoming cargo required inspection, annual costs would still grow at least $10 billion using such a brute-force approach, and the broader costs to the economy would be substantially larger. According to one estimate, the cost of slowing the delivery of imported goods by one day (because of additional security checks) could amount to $7 billion per year.[35]

An alternative suggestion, proposed by Stephen Flynn, former Coast Guard officer and scholar at the Council on Foreign Relations, would be to develop a database for real-time tracking of containers headed toward the United States and to complete much of the inspecting before goods even reached American shores or land borders. It would work largely through the cooperation of shipping and trucking companies as well as overseas port authorities. Companies and ports that implemented tighter security precautions and monitored their own cargo and loading zones would not have to wait in long customs lines when bringing merchandise into the United States. Customs agents could then focus their limited resources on monitoring and inspecting shipments that did not undergo such offshore procedures.[36] The benefits of such an approach are reflected in data on the number of importers. In 2000 almost 500,000 firms imported products. But the top 1,000 importers accounted for almost two-thirds of the imports, highlighting the potential benefits of specialized security and faster customs clearance for such firms.[37]

With this approach, the agency would not have to expand its capabilities tenfold or more. Thus it could selectively target those shipments of goods that posed the greatest risk for inspection at home and rely on good port security and monitoring in overseas ports where U.S.-bound cargo is loaded for most protection, as well as on continuous tracking of cargo in transit using Global Positioning Satellite (GPS) receivers and transmitters.

For the maximum effect, Customs would have to work with the Coast Guard. Potentially dangerous ships and cargo should not be permitted to enter ports near large U.S. cities before being inspected to prevent the dissemination or detonatation of their cargoes. They should be inspected while still at sea, before leaving foreign ports, or in smaller U.S. ports further removed from large population centers. The Coast Guard would have to ensure that such ships did not enter restricted waters. And Customs officials might have to ask some companies to use nonmetal containers to facilitate x-raying and other screening diagnostics.[38]

Customs might therefore need to expand its work force, but only by a factor of perhaps three to five. It might also need to buy new equipment, such as fissile-material detectors and x-ray devices for examining a larger fraction of the total cargo entering the United States. But these needs would not be excessive if cargo could be selectively screened. Despite the huge volumes of cargo entering the United States by ship, about the same amount of equipment being bought for airport security might suffice for the Customs Service as well under the new customs procedures. In round numbers, that might suggest $5 billion in investment costs.[39]

Customs would certainly need a new integrated database system that connected its various offices and agents with the Coast Guard, Immigration and Naturalization Service (INS), and private shipping companies. To judge by the costs of large national-scale information technology systems of comparable scale—for example, the upgrading of Internal Revenue Service (IRS) computer infrastructure in recent years—costs could be $1 billion or more for that part of the effort. In all, the annual budget for Customs would still grow considerably and might even double, but it would not exceed $5 billion on an average yearly basis.

Improve Port Security

To restrict access to the nation by sea also requires strengthening local port security, as documented by the Interagency Commission on Crime and Security in U.S. Seaports. Physical security at the port itself is the responsibility not only of the Coast Guard and Customs, but also of the local port authority and private shipping companies. The most important improvements here include better training and pay for port police and security personnel, a credentialing process to restrict access to secure areas of the ports, greater procedural security for passengers and crew, limits on vehicular traffic around seaports, and additional physical security at the facilities used to handle hazardous materials. In the Coast Guard's estimate, such steps would cost between $14 million and $24 million per port.[40] Improving security at the nation's top 50 ports would therefore cost approximately $1 billion, some of which would represent capital costs that should be depreciated over many years.

Road and Rail

The United States has nearly 6,000 miles of borders with its neighbors, Mexico and Canada.[41] How to prevent terrorists or dangerous materials from entering the country by road or rail is therefore a critical question. The reforms to the Customs Service just mentioned would be helpful, of course, as would changes in the Immigration and Naturalization Service and Border Patrol discussed shortly.

A key way to improve the flow of goods at the nation's land borders would be to adopt the EZ-pass approach there as well: if shippers agreed to more extensive background checks and more intensive security procedures, they would be cleared through customs more rapidly than other shippers. In March 2002, the United States and Mexico announced plans to implement such an EZ-pass approach to their joint border.[42]

People: Ports of Entry

The principal purpose of homeland border security is to prevent any known or suspected terrorists from entering the country and to apprehend any such person if they do attempt entry. To filter the few dangerous people from the many legitimate visitors and others arriving at ports of entry, border officials must be able to ascertain the identity of people seeking to cross our borders, and to link that identity to the risk that the individual may intend to commit a terrorist attack. This means that entry documents should, to the maximum extent possible, not be granted to dangerous individuals; and once such a document is issued, it must be possible to ascertain whether the bearer is in fact the person for whom the entry document was intended.

Three steps can be taken to achieve these goals. First, the process for granting visas must be tightened. Clearly, visas should not be granted to any person identified through solid intelligence, at any level of government, as a threat to the United States. Border agencies and the State Department should also have more access to foreign intelligence on terrorists.[43] Second, visas and passports must be of such a form that fake documents cannot be passed as real, at border crossings, places of employment, or state agencies. Third, officials at entry points must be able to ensure that the document holder and the document match. Efforts to tighten visa processing, document authenticity, and document checks will involve many agencies, including the INS, the State Department, and every level of law enforcement. The effective use of information technology, along with the commitment to share information, can play a crucial role in helping to prevent terrorists from entering the United States without incurring undue economic or social costs.

The quality of information sharing among agencies can be measured by a few broad standards: quantity of information, accuracy (including real time updates), verifiability, and the reliability and speed of the information systems. Ideally, a single database would contain relevant information from each agency, including some biometric identifier that would allow an accurate match of the person, the document held by the person, and any database information about the person. In practice, various constraints—including the difficulties of multiagency cooperation and problems caused by previous underfunding and mismanagement—inhibit such information sharing. To be sure, some progress has been made in this regard. For example, the TIPOFF database, developed after the first World Trade Center attack, shares certain basic identifying information without delving into more sensitive information.[44] But much more aggressive use of information technology is needed to protect the nation's borders.

To return to the all-important visa approval process, the State Department issues immigrant and nonimmigrant visas after checking every applicant's name with consular databases containing records from consular offices and various border and federal law enforcement offices. The Patriot Act directed the Federal Bureau of Investigation (FBI) to share the National Crime Center's Interstate Identification Index with both the State Department and the Immigration and Naturalization Service. This is an improvement on the old system, which only required immigrant visa applicants to be checked on the FBI database. (Legislation that has recently passed in both houses of Congress would further expand database sharing and improve the visa approval process.) It is important that this database be expanded to an all-service system. Performing name checks on a comprehensive database is the single easiest way to filter out dangerous visitors. In addition to strengthening this database, the State Department can improve visa processing in several other ways.

As Mary Ryan, Assistant Secretary for Consular Affairs, has testified, "Consular officers use a combination of experience, knowledge of local economic, political, and cultural conditions and common sense to evaluate applications."[45] Beyond such subjective evaluations, applicants of certain nationalities are automatically subjected to special clearance procedures. After September 11, additional staffing to scrutinize such visa applicants seems warranted. All male nonimmigrant visa applicants between the ages of 16 and 45 must already fill out a supplemental form, and evaluating the honesty of answers can be exceptionally difficult. A January 2001 General Accounting Office (GAO) report listed certain challenges facing State Department visa processing, including "staffing shortages, inexperienced staff, and insufficient training for consular line officers."[46] The $78 million increase in border security programs in the Bush administration's 2003 budget proposal is not an adequate response to the challenge of tightening visa processing.

Not all foreign visitors go through the visa inspection process. Citizens of 28 countries may enter the United States without a visa for stays of less than 90 days through the Visa Waiver Program (VWP). This system has been abused by terrorists and other criminals seeking entry into the country, people who would have been disqualified through the normal visa-issuing process.[47] The government must therefore make a special effort to reduce passport fraud from VWP participant countries. At a minimum, it should ensure that all stolen passports from citizens of VWP countries are entered in the INS database and that all aliens trying to use passports for entry are checked in the lookout database.[48] Stolen passports, or stolen blank passport stock, are often not reported. Law enforcement officials in the United States must work more aggressively with their foreign counterparts in VWP countries to step up such reporting and make certain those countries are meeting the basic requirements of the program. One such requirement is that all VWP countries must adopt machine-readable passports by 2003. The INS recently visited six VWP countries to ensure compliance with the program's rules, and these efforts will continue.[49]

Second, fraud-proof documents are essential to the integrity of the immigration system. Altered or counterfeit documents, some with false names, and shared or borrowed documents from similar-looking individuals, allow people to bypass the protocol of normal visa- or passport-issuing processes. U.S. passports and visas are sophisticated documents with digitized photos, and all visas are machine-readable. Furthermore, the VWP sets standards for passport integrity. Nevertheless, fraud is still a problem. The best way to reduce fraud is to increase the use of biometric identifiers, but this will require additional resources at entry points into the country.

The third step in preventing potential terrorists from entering the country is to match documents at the border. When people arrive at a port of entry—whether they are American citizens, foreign visa holders, or citizens of VWP countries—the INS is responsible for allowing them into the country. The INS conducts more than 500 million inspections every year but employs only 4,775 inspectors to handle this job at all ports of entry.[50] In the short term, additional manpower is probably the best means of tightening inspections at the ports of entry, since it will allow more thorough inspections without costly delays.

Over the longer term, tighter inspections could be achieved with reduced waiting times by including a biometric identifier on all travel documents and building the appropriate infrastructure at every port of entry to capture that identifier both on the document and the person entering the country. Ideally, INS inspectors would know immediately whether the document and the visitor matched, and whether the person was on a lookout list. Face recognition technology could be used with recorded digital photos, and retinal scanners could also be used. Fingerprint technology is rather inexpensive; leaving aside the cost of the databases themselves, it can cost as little as a few dollars to install simple pads for taking fingerprints, and even more complex optical scanners can be made small and affordable.[51] The INS and State Department are trying to quickly expand the use of biometric cards by American, Mexican, and Canadian citizens who frequently cross the border. Some of these efforts could ultimately be joined with parallel efforts in Europe.[52] The basic idea of the EZ-pass approach is to speed up entry through immigration and customs of those who have already undergone thorough background checks and who have proper documentation, and thereby to reduce the costs of homeland security. Counting costs of biometric indicators as well as improved computer systems, costs could be $2 billion or more.

People: Undeveloped Border

Of course, not everyone enters the country through a port of entry. Even with tighter controls at ports of entry, potential terrorists will still be able to cross into the country at points along the unmanned border because it is impossible to achieve complete control over movements across the nearly 6,000 miles of borders the United States shares with Mexico and Canada.[53] Nonetheless, increasing border security can make crossing the border more difficult, especially if resources are directed toward the major gaps in the U.S. border security program.

Checking the border between ports of entry is the task of the U.S. Border Patrol, which has expanded greatly since the mid-1990s. The 2003 budget proposal requests $76 million to add 570 Border Patrol agents, for a total force of over 11,000, as authorized by the 1996 Immigration Reform Law. Since the 1996 statute did not envision as aggressive a counterterrorism role for the Border Patrol as now seems warranted, further expansions in staffing would be beneficial to ensure that the agency can meet the new demands it is facing. To add another 1,000 agents would cost about $150 million per year.

In addition, the Border Patrol's resources should be redirected. Reflecting the pattern of illegal immigration flows, most of the Border Patrol's resources have been concentrated along the southwestern border, making the northern border particularly vulnerable. The INS assigned only 334 Border Patrol agents to the northern border, which does not even allow 24-hour monitoring of certain of its sections.[54] Modern technologies, which include cameras and sensors for surveillance and interdiction, could help the Border Patrol catch people illegally entering from Canada. In November, President George W. Bush released funding for 100 National Guard troops to serve at ports of entry along the northern border, but a more permanent solution is still needed. The 2003 budget proposal would shift 285 agents from the southwestern border to the northern border.

The INS must also improve the architecture of its information technology and the quality of its databases. Currently it does not have the technology to receive all nonimmigrant visa files from the State Department, although State is willing to provide those files.[55] The INS has fallen behind in other information technology initiatives relating to immigration services and the development of an automated entry-exit system. Although the INS has a statutory obligation to record apprehended and criminal aliens in the IDENT database, for example, the Justice Department's Inspector General found that many apprehended and criminal aliens are not entered into the database.[56] Better management and better databases at INS will improve information sharing and help other border agencies filter out individuals known to be dangerous. As at Customs, total capital costs alone could exceed $1 billion just for computer networks.

Given the amount of progress needed to improve processing through ports of entry and the difficulty of patrolling the unmanned border, the United States must coordinate its homeland security efforts with those of Canada and Mexico. It should urge Canada to strengthen its own immigration system, which would offer the best protection against terrorists entering the United States from that country. To increase security along the Mexican border, it may have to help Mexico finance some of the relevant capital costs. Some costs may be incurred in building better coast guards for U.S. neighbors or, at least, in developing integrated databases and in helping train people to use them. In rough terms, given the size of Mexico and its population, U.S. costs might be expected to increase 25 percent to 50 percent in various cases if the United States subsidized part of the Mexico's costs. But such subsidies are not a first order of business; given its diplomatic and legal complexities, it is an issue to consider once the initial steps within the United States have been taken.

Conclusion

The United States has long and porous borders that are virtually impossible to monitor and protect perfectly. But a number of steps can provide layers of imperfect defenses that, when joined together, could make it quite difficult for terrorists to get both themselves and their weapons into the country. Some of these tools, such as improved databases of suspected criminals or individuals who have overstayed their visas, would do more than provide perimeter defense; they would also help find dangerous people once they were already inside the United States.

Some types of perimeter protection, such as national cruise missile defense or a robust and comprehensive customs inspection process for cargo entering the country, may be more costly than their likely benefits. Even so, they merit further scrutiny. Regardless of what decisions are made about those issues, most of the steps proposed in this chapter make good sense and should be adopted. Moreover, while many of them are present in the Bush administration's plans for homeland security, resources are often still inadequate and the scale of planned effort too small.

3

PREVENTIVE MEASURES WITHIN THE UNITED STATES

A single line of defense along the country's borders, while important and worthy of significant improvements, is inadequate in this age of terrorism. The United States needs more than just perimeter defenses to protect itself. Terrorists unknown to the intelligence community could enter the country; terrorists need not be foreigners; weapons could be acquired here, or in some cases sneaked in despite the best efforts of a revamped Customs Service; and other holes in the outer line of defenses would surely exist as well, even after many improvements were carried out.

Even if a terrorist were to evade the nation's perimeter defenses, the likelihood and severity of a successful terrorist attack could be reduced through domestic preventive measures. The goals of such measures should be to find terrorists before they strike and to limit access to weapons that could be used in a terrorist attack, such as pathogens or nuclear or radiological materials. Although preventive measures are not infallible, they are likely to be among the nation's most cost-effective mechanisms for reducing the risk of terrorism, given the inherent advantage of attackers and the fact that protecting some sites will simply displace risk to others. In other words, preventive measures are likely

Table 3-1. *Preventive Measures within the United States*

Area of concern	Measure
Tracking potential terrorists	FBI staffing
	Data sharing among law enforcement agencies
	Surveillance technologies
	Entry and exit data
	Standards for driver's licenses
Tracking and securing dangerous materials	Hazardous materials shipments
	Natural gas facilities
	Chemical/oil/gas plants
	Dangerous pathogens
	Nuclear weapons and waste

to be particularly effective because they tend to reduce overall levels of risk, rather than just shifting it from one target to another. Tables 3-1 and 3-2 present an agenda for improving domestic prevention against terrorist activity.

The challenge of interdicting terrorists before they can act centers around the effective mobilization of information. This is a fivefold task:

—*collecting* information that can help identify terrorists;

—*collating* information from diverse sources;

—*analyzing* raw data;

—*sharing* the information with those who can make use of it; and

—*deploying* it in a way that is useful and timely for those who need to act on it.

Although significant resources are devoted to each of these tasks today, and the administration's proposals would enhance capabilities in many areas, there remain serious shortfalls in each of these areas. Equally important, we lack an overall architecture to make sure that each component of the information strategy is integrated in a way to achieve the intended goals. Massive information collection will potentially be quite intrusive yet of little value if it is not shared in a usable way with key consumers (border inspectors, airline screeners, employers at sensitive facilities). Widely shared raw data will be of little help unless it is collated and combined

Table 3-2. *Proposals to Buttress Preventive Measures within the United States*

Area of concern	Specific measure	Approximate annual cost[a] (billions of dollars)
Preferred options		
Tracking potential terrorists	Expand INS, FBI, other agencies, and improve monitoring and enforcement of visa limitations	2.5
	Law enforcement and immigration IT initiatives —Expand data sharing —Develop and deploy advanced surveillance and data analysis technologies —Automate entry and exit data[b]	2.0
	Standardize drivers' license databases; consider biometric information	0.2
Tracking and securing dangerous materials	Equip trucks with tracking technology and automatic braking technology	1.0
	Relocate, secure some natural gas assets	0.1
	Protect toxic chemical plants and nuclear facilities with better sensors and guards	5.0
	Increase screening of individuals with access to sensitive materials, pathogens, Internet domains; improve site security at labs, etc.	0.75
	Total low/modest cost	11.55

a. Annual cost relative to original pre-9/11 2002 budget.
b. Denotes similar initiative of comparable magnitude proposed by the Bush administration.

to form profiles that generate high accuracy (low false positives and false negatives). Otherwise, we may impose high economic and human costs for marginal gains.

In this chapter we propose several measures both to strengthen each component of the prevention strategy and to integrate them. Further work in this area is the focus of a new Task Force on Security in an Information Age, led by the Markle Foundation in alliance with the Brookings

Institution and the Center for Strategic and International Studies (CSIS). We expect that this task force will substantially deepen our understanding of how to mobilize information for homeland security, especially with respect to the challenge of prevention.

Expand FBI Staffing

The FBI has a crucial role to play in prevention. It is one of the core agencies involved in collecting information about potential terrorists (along with foreign intelligence, state and local officials, and the private sector). It is one of the principal consumers of the analysis effort. Through the National Crime Information Center (NCIC), the Integrated Automated Fingerprint Identification System (IAFIS), and Law Enforcement On-Line (LEO), it is a focal point for collating and analysis. And as a law enforcement agency, it is an essential user of information for law enforcement purposes. Before the September 11 attacks, roughly 25 percent of the FBI's nearly 9,000 special agents in the field were assigned to counterintelligence or counterterrorism duties. Following the September 11 attacks and the subsequent anthrax scare, the FBI shifted several thousand agents to terrorism-related activities.[1] To properly staff counterterrorism efforts while avoiding severe understaffing in other areas, the FBI needs to expand its manpower.

The Bush administration has proposed increasing FBI counterterrorist staffing by about 450 individuals.[2] We believe that much larger expansions may be required. In December 2001, for example, the FBI was using 3,000 more agents for counterterrorism purposes than it had budgeted.[3] Furthermore, the General Accounting Office has indicated that the FBI may lack sufficient numbers of trained translators and interpreters; such positions are crucial to an effective counterterrorism team, and it is unclear to what extent the Bush administration's proposals address any such gap.[4] Devoting 5,000 agents, analysts, and language specialists to counterterrorism and counterintelligence—which would cost perhaps $750 million to $1 billion a year, assuming an average cost per agent (including salary, benefits, training, equipment, and other costs) of up to $200,000—seems warranted. In particular, we support an increase in FBI staffing of 1,000 per year for the next five years, so that staffing would increase by 5,000 by the fifth year in relation to today.

State and Local Government Law Enforcement Officials

Even with a substantial expansion of the FBI, the task of information collection, surveillance, and law enforcement can be significantly enhanced by the better use of state and local law enforcement officers. Here the challenge is less a question of manpower than training and support resources: training to recognize information and behavior that may help identify potential terrorists, means of sharing that information with other local and federal officials, and means of receiving timely useful information from others that would allow the apprehension or interdiction of potential perpetrators.

To date, most of the focus of effort with respect to state and local law enforcement officials has been on consequence management. State and local law enforcement officials have repeatedly complained about lack of access to relevant data, resulting from inadequate systems, compartmentalization based on security concerns, and failure to appreciate the role of local officials. A new priority in this area would be to focus primarily on training and information management systems.

Private Sector

The private sector possesses troves of information that may be of value to the prevention effort—ranging from Internet service providers (ISP) and telecommunications companies with records about dangerous hackers and intruders to employers with workplace information on employees, to sellers of potentially hazardous materials and services (for example, crop duster rental firms). The challenge here is enormous: to cull, collate, and analyze extraordinary amounts of data in a way that is cost-effective and sensitive to civil liberties concerns in order to identify high-impact strategies with adequate privacy safeguards. A public-private partnership, modeled on the collaboration between the federal government and the private sector for cybersecurity protection, such as Carnegie Mellon's Computer Emergency Response Team Coordination Center (CERT/CC), should be developed for key private sector holders of information that could have a high degree of relevance to the identification of potential terrorists. Adequate legal supervision (for example, court orders or senior official approvals to permit information sharing) will be crucial.

Data Collection and Data Analysis Technologies

The information revolution has both radically expanded the range and availability of information and complicated the technical and analytical challenge of using it. The wiretap of yesteryear was a simple proposition: identify a suspect's phone and listen to conversations. In an age of wireless, packet-switched, encrypted communication, the challenge is much more daunting. In recent years, both the private sector and government have substantially increased their ability to collect and analyze data from a wide array of services. The FBI has developed an application, initially called Carnivore but more recently renamed DCS 1000, that can search e-mail traffic for specific senders, recipients, and keywords. Another technology, Magic Lantern, can surreptitiously record keystrokes on targeted computers, thus circumventing the use of strong encryption. Similar advances have been made in collecting and analyzing information, from sophisticated data-mining software to technologies such as face recognition software that matches digital images of faces to suspects in a database.[5] These technologies offer a promising approach to tracking and apprehending terrorists before they actually strike, and substantial expansion in the development and application of such technologies represents a sound strategy for protecting the homeland. To be sure, they also raise important privacy issues, although the technologies themselves may be configured in ways that will enhance their privacy protection features. Carefully done, the benefits of sophisticated use of information technologies for collection and analysis to reduce the risks of terrorism justify an increased focus, especially given proper control over access to the raw data and how it is used.

Automated Entry and Exit Data

Even without a dramatic expansion in monitoring and data mining, several steps could be taken to better enforce existing laws and thereby reduce opportunities for terrorists to operate in the country. For example, the U.S. government does not have reliable data on whether a visitor or visa holder is in the country or has departed. The Immigration and Naturalization Service estimates that 40 to 50 percent of illegal immigrants in the United States entered the country legally but overstayed their visas.[6] Several factors hinder the collection of entry-exit data: the task is not automated, airlines sometimes fail to collect data when visitors leave the country, and the government collects no data on land departures. Under the 1996 Illegal Immigration and Immigration Responsibility Act, the INS is required to automate the collection of I-94 forms, but a limited pilot program begun in 1997 has been by and large unsuccessful.[7] In 2000, Congress extended its deadlines for automating I-94 collections to 2003 at airports and seaports, and to 2005 at all ports of entry.

The slow progress in automating I-94 forms may be symptomatic of larger managerial problems at the INS, especially with respect to managing information technology. The General Accounting Office released two reports in 2000 criticizing the oversight, management, and allocation of investments in information technology at INS.[8]

New technology will be useful for managing other information about visa holders. Congress has set a deadline of January 2003 for implementation of the Student Exchange Visitor Information System (SEVIS), which will track student visa holders. The government could also require visa sponsors to report annually on the status of the visa holders.

Even if the government possessed reliable information on visa overstays, the relevant agencies do not currently have the resources to make full use of it. With only 2,000 investigators and intelligence agents, INS resources are already overextended, and any new initiatives to enforce immigration laws aggressively would likely require additional resources. Some improvements could be made without increased staffing; for example (as suggested earlier), giving local law enforcement officers access to federal databases could help them find individuals who no longer belong in the country. Local agencies may then need help with investments in information systems. Certain agencies, including but not limited to the INS and the FBI, will have to increase in size if they are to accumulate and process more data as well, as discussed in chapter 2. Given the modest sizes of most of these agencies, even rapid growth rates in their staffs are unlikely to be enormously costly. Adding 10,000 personnel would translate into roughly $1.5 billion in added annual costs, not an unreasonable amount.

Improved Data Sharing

The problem of lack of information sharing and collating of immigration data is symptomatic of the broad need for enhanced data sharing between all key collectors and users. The FBI is already taking steps to better share information from its Integrated Automated Fingerprint Identification System, the National Crime Information Center, and Law Enforcement On-Line.[9] But significant problems remain. For one thing, the NCIC does not contain information about immigration status or minor crimes, and state and local law enforcement authorities often fail to enter the relevant data into the database in a timely fashion.[10] The government should also move more aggressively to tie together currently disparate data sources, as the lack of integration between immigration and criminal records highlights. A massive effort to link such databases, which are often run by currently incompatible systems, as well as to expand the use of handheld computers by law enforcement agents (including state and local personnel), may require several billions of dollars in hardware investments, along with substantial software expenditures.

In addition, policymakers should introduce measures to expand data sharing between government agencies and private sector entities. Such data sharing could occur on a "need-to-know" basis, to minimize concerns about civil liberty and privacy intrusions. For example, as Tim Hoescht, the senior vice president for technology at Oracle, has noted, improved data sharing "doesn't mean it'll be a free-for-all of systems access. . . . Such access will be regulated by policymakers just as it is today. Policymakers may decide that it is appropriate for airlines to check if a passenger is on a terrorist watch list but that it's not okay for them to check whether they have unpaid parking tickets."[11] In our opinion, policymakers should encourage greater data sharing among law enforcement agencies and between the government and appropriate private sector firms, even if it necessitates changes to the Privacy Act of 1974 (as amended by the Computer Matching and Privacy Protection Act of 1988) and despite the potential civil liberty and privacy concerns it raises.

Unified and Strengthened Standards for Obtaining Driver's Licenses

An important link in the nexus between information strategies and prevention is the driver's license, which has effectively become the primary form of identification in the United States.[12] Driver's licenses (or other related identification cards) are issued by states and are generally accepted in other states as valid identification. Yet the rules for issuing them—such as the definition of residency—vary substantially across the states.[13] Seven of the September 11 terrorists were able to obtain Virginia driver's licenses even though they did not live in the state, and those licenses then allowed them to board airplanes, use credit cards, and open bank accounts.[14] To reduce the number of fraudulent licenses and make it more difficult for potential terrorists to operate in the United States, the standards used to issue licenses should be coordinated across the states, the licenses themselves should contain biometric information and a digitized photo, and national databases (such as the Driver Record Information Verification System) should be created to facilitate information sharing among local, state, and Federal agencies.

According to the American Association of Motor Vehicle Administrators, it would cost about $60 million to establish a national database for driver's licenses: $10 million for the database, $25 million for states to implement one or more biometric identifiers, and a one-time cost of $500,000 per state to connect to the database.[15] This estimate seems low and incomplete alongside others. Hong Kong, for example, plans to issue an enhanced identification card for its population of 6 million at a cost about $400 million. Even if efficiencies and economies of scale are possible here, one might expect costs to approach $5 billion or more. According to other estimates, a single airport or other major facility handling large amounts of human traffic could need $1 million in infrastructure to read biometric signatures (especially if it was using retinal scanners). By this reckoning as well, $25 million could easily be the cost per state, and the overall national requirement could total in the low billions of dollars.[16]

Implementing a broader plan to mandate a national identity card might cost $10 billion or more. We believe that there is a strong argument for considering such a card, rather than relying on a patchwork of state-run driver's licenses that do not extend to the entire population

Addressing Concerns over Privacy and Civil Liberties

Many public interest groups on both sides of the political spectrum complain that the types of steps advocated here, including expanded data sharing and uniform standards for state driver's licenses, risk infringing on a citizen's privacy and "would facilitate the creation of the surveillance society that Americans have always resisted."[17] Expanded data sharing and a single individual identifier, they argue, would collect vast amounts of information on innocent individuals with little or no relevance to deterring or preventing terrorism, would allow heretofore unorganized information to be consolidated into "big brother" practices, and could be used for purposes unrelated to the prevention of terrorism. Such concerns have some validity; but they should not prevent the nation from more aggressively using information technologies to reduce the risk of terrorism. Rather, the challenge is to devise strategies that would allow more effective mobilization of information strategies while securing essential privacy.

One set of concerns involves increased data sharing with nongovernment entities. Here the government could permit access to public databases only for legitimate purposes, through authorization controls that could selectively compartmentalize information. Queries to databases need not necessarily retrieve all the underlying information; a "need-to-know" criterion is crucial. An airline representative could legitimately gain access to information on prior convictions on immigration violations or presence on a watch list that would justify more intense scrutiny, but would not need "all information on John Doe." Information exchange between the public sector and the private sector would still be limited to legitimate needs, such as background checks for sensitive employees.

Information sharing even among government agencies, especially in law enforcement, has also been a matter of great concern. Linking distributed databases would not necessarily give an official access to any and all information, but it would reduce the cost and time involved in such access. In some cases, however, moving to the expanded use of information technologies and electronic records could also *improve* privacy protections, since it is often easier to monitor how officials access and use electronic records than it is to track such use of paper records.[18] Building in further protections, such as court supervision of collection methods and use, can also contribute to enhancing privacy protection.

Tracking and Securing Dangerous Materials

Domestic prevention also means restricting access to materials that can be used in a terrorist attack. Weapons of mass destruction—nuclear, radiological, chemical, and biological—pose the most lethal threat to the American population, and therefore special precautions should be undertaken to protect and track materials that could be used in such weapons. But weapons of mass destruction are not the only concern. Conventional explosives can kill or threaten Americans in considerable numbers, as evidenced by the Oklahoma City bombing, the 1993 attack on the World Trade Center, the subsequent plot by Ramzi Yousef to blow up 11 airliners over the Pacific around 1994, the 1996 Khobar Towers bombing in Saudi Arabia, the 1998 embassy bombings in Africa, and the 2000 bombing of the U.S.S. destroyer *Cole*. And of course, it was the combination of aircraft impact and the resulting fires that killed more than 3,000 on September 11, mostly at the World Trade Center. Several steps can be taken to restrict access to potential weapons.

Regulate and Track Hazardous Shipments

Hazardous and explosive materials represent potential ingredients of a terrorist attack. In the United States, the majority of these materials are transported by trucks, which often travel near populated centers.[19] Roughly 800,000 hazardous materials shipments by truck occur each day, and about 5 percent of total truck mileage involves such shipments.[20]

Three essential steps can be taken to protect such shipments from being captured or used by terrorists. First, better screening is needed for those authorized to drive the trucks. Individuals on terrorist watch lists, illegal aliens, and some categories of criminals should not be allowed to operate these vehicles. Second, trucks carrying especially dangerous materials in sensitive areas should have safety features that would prevent anyone from tampering with their cargo, would alert authorities to any change in their routes, and allow them to be stopped if they did divert from their proper route.[21] Third, security at plants and storage depots must be substantially improved. Hazardous materials have often been left in preloaded trailers in nonsecure lots before being picked up by trucking firms. Such practices should not continue.[22]

Like some shippers clearing Customs, trucking firms might qualify for an "EZ-pass" as part of a tighter security system. Such firms would undertake detailed background checks of drivers and would have biometric features to ensure that only approved drivers operate trucks carrying hazardous materials. The firms could also introduce GPS monitoring of truck movements, remote disabling systems to stop a truck that had been hijacked, and other remote monitoring systems for cargo integrity. These and other criteria would govern access to some populated areas or highways that unapproved trucking firms were not allowed to enter. Such a system would provide an economic incentive for implementing stronger security measures, which might cost $1,000 per truck if done rigorously, or hundreds of millions of dollars nationwide.

Shipping by rail poses certain concerns as well. Chlorine, for example, a toxic chemical that can enhance the combustion of other substances, is often stored and shipped in 90-ton rail tank cars. A release of 90 tons of chlorine could affect populations up to 14 miles away.[23] Similar security measures to those adopted for trucks with dangerous cargoes should therefore be considered.

Relocate Parts of the Natural Gas Infrastructure

It may be prudent to relocate parts of the infrastructure that carries natural gas and other dangerous materials. Where an explosion or leak could kill thousands and where stations cannot easily be protected, serious consideration should be given to burying or moving the structure in question. This could be a massive task, especially if it involved relocating pipelines. However, most pipelines already appear to be fairly secure (and the Office of Pipeline Safety within the Department of Transportation has been undertaking additional steps to make them even more secure), so the problem is limited to a small number of individual cases, generally involving not the pipelines themselves but loading and offloading facilities.

In one case, a proposal to reopen a liquid natural gas plant in a region of Maryland's Chesapeake Bay shore at a cost of $120 million has met with sharp criticism. Residents and lawmakers alike fear that a ship carrying gas to the facility could be detonated and then cause an explosion at a nearby nuclear power plant.[24] In such cases, existing facilities might need to be replaced; the above cost figure may be a representative estimate of the expenditures that would be required. Given the difficulty of transporting natural gas, the government's primary concern should be to prevent explosions near highly populated areas or facilities such as nuclear plants—not to protect the entire natural gas production and distribution system.

Improve Security at Chemical Plants

Attacks against major chemical plants near cities could impose particularly high costs and huge casualty figures. Some suggested scenarios, with tens or even hundreds of thousands of possible deaths, could make the 1984 Bhopal disaster in India, in which some 2,000 died, pale by comparison. The United States has roughly 12,000 chemical facilities.[25] Many of these facilities do not pose dangers themselves, and the vast majority of worst-case scenarios involving flammable chemical facilities, for example, would not affect significant population centers.[26] On the other hand, large quantities of dangerous materials could be stolen from such facilities. Furthermore, the majority of worst-case scenarios involving toxic chemicals (such as ammonia and chlorine) would affect areas with residential populations of 10,000 or more.[27] According to an Environmental Protection Agency report, at least 123 U.S. plants store toxic chemicals that, if released, could endanger one million people or more. An Army Surgeon General's report suggests that casualties could be even higher than one million.[28]

Security at many chemical facilities has not been sufficient, as demonstrated even before September 11 by environmentalists from Greenpeace. They were able to enter a Dow Chemical plant in Louisiana without being detected and claimed that there were no guards on the perimeter, no security cameras, no alarms, and that the door was even unlocked.[29] That plant was apparently capable of releasing significant amounts of hydrogen chloride, which could have threatened hundreds of thousands of people.[30] To beef up the typical security effort with several dozen more personnel and much better remote monitoring equipment, each chemical firm might spend a few million dollars a year, making for a national cost of several billion dollars.[31] These costs should be borne by the chemical firms themselves (see chapter 6); insurance companies could play some role in providing incentives for even better security measures at chemical facilities.

Limit Access to Dangerous Pathogens

The security surrounding dangerous biological pathogens has improved since the Antiterrorist and Effective Death Penalty Act was passed in 1996. Under that law, the Department of Health and Human Services requires facilities that handle any of 42 dangerous biological agents to register with the government and to disclose the purpose of having such agents. Yet the existing program covers only about 250 laboratories in the United States out of the more than 550 laboratories that hold some quantity of the dangerous agents.[32] Furthermore, the 1996 law does not impose criminal penalties on nonscientists who possess dangerous pathogens, nor does it require background checks for all lab workers.[33] These loopholes need to be closed.

To prevent terrorists from obtaining and using dangerous pathogens, laboratories need to have maximum physical security and require background checks for all scientists, technicians, and other lab workers with access to potentially dangerous materials. Security at labs might typically cost $1 million, while background checks for employees might cost $100,000 (assuming several days' work per person for a work force of perhaps 100). Criminal penalties should be imposed on those who improperly obtain or possess dangerous pathogens. And local law enforcement officials should closely monitor potential delivery mechanisms (such as crop dusters and large fans).

Improve Nuclear Security

Security should be particularly tight at the nation's 103 nuclear power plants, which supply close to 20 percent of the nation's electricity and which contain materials that could be used to produce a primitive nuclear device or perhaps a radiological or "dirty" bomb.[34] (A dirty bomb would not produce a nuclear reaction but would spread radioactive materials over a wide area.) Nuclear power plants are plagued by two vulnerabilities. An attack on a power plant could be catastrophic, leading to the deaths of thousands or even tens of thousands.[35] At the same time, the fuel used in nuclear power plants could be used in a dirty bomb or processed into a nuclear weapon. Other parts of the nuclear fuel cycle—such as fuel enrichment and fabrication and waste-reprocessing plants—face similar or perhaps even greater vulnerabilities.

To improve security and limit access to nuclear fuel before, during, and after it is used in a power reactor, the Nuclear Regulatory Commission (NRC) should enforce tighter background checks on all employees with access to nuclear materials and should prohibit such access until the check is completed. In some instances, notes the Union of Concerned Scientists, workers have been granted access to nuclear facilities while awaiting the results of these security checks.[36] Furthermore, the initial background checks are limited to the United States; as the NRC has noted, "U.S. citizens are currently accounted for better than foreign applicants, due to the lack of information (e.g., credit history and criminal history) or unwillingness of the [foreign] country to provide such information."[37] This shortcoming needs to be addressed. After the initial background check, the NRC should better enforce screening procedures at all nuclear facilities, including those that have ceased operations but continue to house dangerous materials.[38]

In addition, nuclear facilities should conduct more rigorous security exercises under the Safeguards Performance Assessment and Operational Safeguards Response Evaluation programs.[39] Two particularly important scenarios to consider in these exercises are that the plant's connection to the electricity grid could be interrupted during the attack, and that the mock intruders could ally with an "insider" at the plant. Some reactors may also require improved physical protection or additional security measures, especially to withstand attacks by air or sea, and not only four-wheel-drive land-vehicle bombs, up to now the main concern of most regulations.[40]

Spent fuel represents a particular vulnerability. One recent press report suggests that security may be unduly lax at the Maine Yankee Nuclear Power Station, which is no longer operational but which stores more spent nuclear fuel than any other decommissioned power plant in the United States.[41] Other reports suggest that spent fuel at operating power plants is not protected sufficiently, and that an attack using such fuel could cause thousands of deaths.[42] To improve the security of spent fuel, the NRC should reexamine its regulations, and the Department of Energy should accelerate its plans to provide secure storage of spent nuclear fuel, even if a permanent repository is not quickly made operational.

The NRC recently issued new regulations enhancing security at nuclear power plants, but their adequacy is impossible to assess from the open literature. These measures are classified information, but according to an NRC press release they pertain mainly to security patrols, physical barriers, coordination with law enforcement and the military, and controls over vehicular and personnel access. Whatever their adequacy, it is essential that such regulations be enforced.

Legislative changes could also help thwart terrorists. The NRC has already taken one step along these lines: it has proposed the Atomic Energy

Act add measures specifying that the unauthorized presence of weapons or explosives at nuclear facilities would be subject to federal criminal penalties, and that guards at the facilities would be allowed to have weapons similar to those used by federal protective forces.[43]

Costs for tightening security at nuclear plants and other components of the nuclear fuel cycle are difficult to estimate without a detailed analysis of the required improvements or remedial action, but that is beyond the scope of this book. To arrive at a rough estimate, however, we can assume that each of the country's reactors and waste facilities could be mandated to undertake security improvements at least on a par with those discussed earlier for large chemical plants. In that event, one-time costs could be about $1 billion and added annual costs again as much. Such costs should be borne by the consumers and shareholders of the facilities. The idea of using thousands of National Guard troops for such purposes, as has been the case since September 11, is not defensible over the longer term given the other responsibilities of the National Guard and the nuclear industry's responsibility to provide its own protection.

Conclusion

In the absence of specific information about potential targets, a particularly cost-effective way to reduce the risks of homeland terrorist activity is to undertake preventive measures such as improved surveillance of potential terrorists and better protection of weapons or dangerous materials that could be used by terrorists. Such measures supplement the perimeter defense steps outlined in chapter 2, providing an additional layer of security to frustrate potential terrorist activity. In particular, a more systematic effort to integrate collection, collation, analysis, dissemination, and utilization of information on potential terrorists could pay large dividends. Although some preventive measures may raise concerns about civil liberties and privacy, the security benefits of the measures proposed here justify their implementation. Yet Bush administration plans do not yet go far enough in most of these areas. Of course, preventive measures have their own limitations. Chapter 4 therefore explores how the nation can protect key targets against attack, should perimeter defense and domestic prevention measures fail to do so fully.

4

PROTECTING TARGETS WITHIN THE UNITED STATES

To ensure adequate homeland security, the preventive measures discussed to this point—limiting access to the country, tracking terrorists, and protecting materials that could be used in a terrorist attack—must be supplemented with the protection of the targets themselves. Protection poses two key problems—the nearly infinite number of feasible targets and the fact that protecting some sites might simply shift risk to other unprotected targets, thus negating much or all of the benefit despite significant costs. Given this displacement effect, we argue that the priority should be to protect targets where a successful attack would impose substantial national costs. A protective strategy should help to deflect terrorist activity from catastrophic settings to less damaging ones, rather than from one catastrophic setting to another. And even if a protective strategy cannot guarantee success against all catastrophic attacks, it should raise the threshold of competence, capability, and inventiveness that terrorists would need to carry out a successful attack.

Numerous steps have already been taken to reduce the odds of a large explosive device being used against the nation and to prevent airplanes from being turned into flying bombs, as they were on September 11. In addition, guards have been stationed around key facilities and buildings, truck traffic and parking has been curtailed near critical parts of the national infrastructure, and vehicle inspections have been intensified near approaches to tunnels and bridges. As of late 2001, about 6,000 military reservists had been deployed to provide airport security, and another 5,500 or so were guarding other critical infrastructure.

This chapter focuses on how the nation can reorient its protection of domestic targets to further reduce the risks of damage to key national interests. Table 4-1 lists the major areas of vulnerability, and table 4-2 presents our options for addressing them.

Targets That Pose Risk of Large-Scale Casualties

The first priority is to protect those targets where large numbers of lives could be lost. They include nuclear and chemical facilities, large commercial buildings and arenas, large national events, and some parts of the infrastructure, such as bridges, tunnels, and subway systems (see the section on infrastructure).[1] Since the federal government has already devised strategies to provide additional security at important national events, such as the recent Olympics, little further effort may be needed in these areas.

Table 4-1. *Protection of Key Targets*

General target	Specific target
Buildings and facilities that could involve large numbers of casualties	Nuclear and chemical facilities Commercial buildings and arenas National events Major tunnels and bridges Aircraft
National symbols	Government buildings and monuments
Critical infrastructure	Airports, trains, and subways Electricity grid, water supply, and mail service Food safety Telecommunications, Internet, and Global Positioning Satellite (GPS) system

Table 4-2. *Means of Improving Protection of Key Targets*

Target of concern	Specific measure	Approximate annual cost[a] (billions of dollars)
Preferred options		
Buildings and facilities with large numbers of people	Improve air intake system security at major nonfederal buildings: accessibility, filters, and reverse pressure/internal overpressure	2.0
	Selectively institute more security precautions at major buildings against conventional explosives (for example, shatterproof glass)	0.5
National symbols	Accelerate GSA plan for federal building security[b]	0.5
	Protect national monuments[b]	0.1
Critical infrastructure	Protect key nodes of electricity grid	0.2
	Place chemical sensors at reservoirs; protect and monitor reservoir grounds and pumps	0.4
	Improve security of mail[b] (10-year annual average)	0.5
	Centralize, bolster food safety inspections	0.25
	Improve cybersecurity clearinghouse; add private sector red team requirements[b]	0.1
	Improve research on cyberprotection, provide scholarships[b]	0.1
	Improve airport security[b]	3.3
	Improve Amtrak security at tunnels, elsewhere	0.1
	Place chemical weapons sensors at many public sites such as subway stations	0.25
	Improve fire resiliency of major tunnels and security at major bridges	0.5
	Total low/modest cost	8.8
Higher-cost/least-risk further options	Hasten deployment of more robust, jam-resistant GPS satellites	0.5

a. Annual cost relative to original pre-9/11 2002 budget.

b. Denotes similar initiative of comparable magnitude proposed by the Bush administration.

Nuclear and Chemical Facilities

As suggested in chapter 3, an attack on a nuclear facility or a plant containing toxic chemicals could result in thousands, if not millions, of deaths and injuries. That is but one reason for protecting them; they also contain dangerous materials that could be used by terrorists to attack other targets. The proposals discussed in chapter 3 for protecting nuclear and chemical facilities against unauthorized entry and theft of materials apply in most cases to the facilities themselves and need not be repeated here. It may be worth noting one step that could be taken to defend against aerial attack: placing steel towers around the site to destroy any plane entering the immediate neighborhood. Such an idea may not be necessary but would address the vulnerability problem fairly inexpensively and reliably.[2]

Large Buildings and Arenas

Beyond the physical protection of large buildings, air intake systems of many major buildings and other infrastructure are an Achilles' heel for this nation. Many are accessible and exposed, so a terrorist armed with a modest amount of biological or chemical agent could readily disperse that agent throughout a building. Moreover, most buildings lack the types of filters that could clean up contamination that does get into the system, either from deliberate attack or from an agent released on a street or from a nearby structure. Few buildings and other large structures are equipped to keep out dangerous air particles that may be in the vicinity.

A first step toward guarding against this threat would be to make air intakes on major buildings as inaccessible to terrorists as possible. In some cases, this may require little more than locking doors previously left open. In other cases, protective housing of one sort or another may need to be constructed to block access. In still others, air intake systems might be relocated, particularly at times when they are being replaced anyway. We are assuming that most air intake systems on existing buildings could be made harder to approach at a modest cost, typically for no more than tens of thousands or hundreds of thousands of dollars per building. (Insurance companies could provide incentives for adopting the more costly approach of relocating systems or replacing existing air and heat systems to accommodate the finest class of air filters.) Second, whenever feasible, large buildings should maintain slight overpressure relative to the outside air to keep out agents that might have been released in the vicinity of a given building and that could seep through cracks and other openings into its interior. Third, some buildings could install filter systems with the capacity to cut down the distribution of such agents that might get into a building by a factor of two to ten.[3]

However, it would be far too expensive to try to adopt such measures for every major structure in the United States, including its 4.6 million commercial buildings, as well as apartment buildings and major public buildings.[4] Attacks on the vast majority of commercial buildings would not involve massive loss of life, for 99 percent of them house fewer than 250 workers, and only 0.2 percent have 10 or more floors.[5] At the same time, the largest of the nation's commercial buildings would probably find the measures presented above cost-effective. According to Michael Janus of Battelle, air filtering systems would cost from less than $100,000 to $400,000 for a building holding 500 people.[6] If the measures were limited to the nation's 500 or so skyscrapers, each with an average occupancy of perhaps 5,000 people, costs might be about $1 billion.[7] The need to replace a certain percentage of filtering systems thereafter, as well as routine maintenance, might imply annual costs of several hundred million dollars.

Tougher building safety codes offer another avenue of protection, especially in new commercial buildings. They should focus on structural integrity, minimizing the probability of collapse even after an explosive attack, and making the buildings more resistant to fire. The National Institute of Standards and Technology, a part of the Department of Commerce, recently proposed adopting lessons from the Department of Defense's "immune buildings" program to develop standards for commercial buildings.[8] Given the costs associated with "hardening" new buildings and the trade-off between risk and cost, any such "anti-terrorism" building codes should probably apply only to the largest new structures, those that would hold thousands of people.[9]

Similar precautions should be taken at major arenas and stadiums. There are roughly 250 major arenas and stadiums in the United States, including those designed for professional athletics, racing, and collegiate sports.[10] Protecting the air intake systems (for the indoor stadiums) and otherwise hardening these structures could cost about $1 billion. Given the occupancy levels of many major arenas, such steps would appear to be crucial in protecting against high-cost terrorist attacks.

As argued in chapter 6, basic improvements in building safety for the nation's largest buildings should be implemented through regulation rather than through federal expenditures or subsidies. The costs would thus be borne by the owners and occupants of the buildings and arenas rather than by the federal government. Such a stakeholder-pays approach would reduce the burden on the federal budget, avoid gold plating of security precautions, and make the real costs of large buildings transparent. In addition, over the longer term, insurance companies could play an important role in providing incentives for additional security precautions, for example, by offering lower insurance premiums to firms willing to install the finest air filters or shatterproof glass in their buildings.

Targets with Significant National Symbolism

Certain monuments, major government buildings, and other national symbols warrant high levels of protection against terrorist attack. Terrorists themselves place high value on attacking such targets (as can be seen from the attack on the Pentagon) because terrorists are often seeking to make a political statement and such a target enhances the publicity associated with the attack, underscores our inability to protect even obvious targets, and thus risks damaging national prestige. Such targets are limited in number, in many cases are irreplaceable, and any damage to them could have a significant adverse psychological impact on the nation. Conversely, thwarting such attacks could discourage some terrorists with political motivations.

Prominent Public Buildings

The federal government has paid much greater attention to its building security since the mid-1990s. After the Oklahoma City bombing, the Justice Department assembled an interagency working group to examine federal building security and develop minimum standards for security. These standards pertain to vehicular access, employee and visitor access, inspections of visitors and employees at entrances, video monitoring of the buildings and grounds, and security patrols. The General Services Administration has funded these improvements, and annual spending for federal building security has tripled since fiscal 1994.

Despite these improvements, significant security gaps remain, especially because security procedures are often ignored. In 2000, for example, GAO undercover agents infiltrated 19 federal building posing as police carrying weapons and a large briefcase. A GSA internal audit found that in many instances contracted security guards at federal buildings never received proper background checks or weapons training.[11] Reporters too have exposed various security lapses at federal government buildings in Washington, even after the September 11 attacks.[12] Part of the problem is that the lowest-bidding private security firm is chosen to staff security checkpoints at most federal buildings. Contracts with such firms should include financial penalties for failing to perform well on unannounced security tests. Alternatively, using government employees as security guards may help to improve safety. To reduce both vulnerability and possible damages from a successful attack, the GSA's five-year security improvement plan for 2001–05 includes capital expenditures totaling $2.3 billion. Among other things, these would cover blast mitigation, surveillance, and chemical and biological detection equipment for ventilation systems.[13]

National Monuments

The federal government is responsible for protecting not only its own buildings but also our national monuments.[14] Of the nation's 29 memorials and 75 national monuments, the 10 or so that are most visible, including the monuments in Washington, D.C., and the Statute of Liberty, require extra security after September 11. These high-risk targets have many visitors every year. Heightened security measures—already in place at many monuments—include more security staff, restricting vehicular access, and implementing thorough visitor screening. The 2003 budget proposal requests a $12 million increase for the National Park Police and physical security improvements at monuments in Washington totaling $30 million. These expansions are of the right rough size to protect the most symbolic national targets, although some additional funds may be needed.

Critical Infrastructure

Given the costs associated with protecting all aspects of the nation's infrastructure, protective measures should focus in part on "single-node" facilities that would be the source of substantial economic and social costs after an

attack and would be difficult to replace in a timely fashion. Equally important are infrastructure failures that would threaten large numbers of lives.

Critical Economic and Social Infrastructure

Expanded security is warranted for numerous aspects of the nation's critical infrastructure, including the electricity grid, the water supply, the food
supply, and the Postal Service. Presidential Decision Directive 63 (PDD-63)
designated key agencies to oversee the protection of critical national infrastructure, but many observers complained that the resultant apparatus was
ineffective. Although the Office of Homeland Security now has broad
supervision over this issue, it still needs closer attention.[15]

To illustrate, suppose that terrorists attacked the electricity grid.
Although experts argue that a coordinated attack on multiple targets would
be required to cause substantial disruptions in the grid as a whole, substa-
tions, generation facilities, and transmission lines remain vulnerable.[16]
According to a leading industry official, "A lot of what can be done simply
involves getting more eyes on the system."[17] But better fencing, monitoring
devices, and other equipment would also help. In addition, the dramatically
expanded use of Supervisory Control and Data Acquisition (SCADA) electronic systems to control energy flows exposes the broader energy sector to
cyberattack.[18] Some of the measures discussed in this chapter to improve
cybersecurity may therefore be particularly relevant to the energy industry.

What costs would be associated with such steps? Electricity-generating
and switching stations are the main points of vulnerability. Downed power
lines are not too difficult to repair, and so will not disrupt life in general or
the economy very much. Since terrorists would have considerable difficulty
causing mass casualties or pervasive economic costs by bringing down a
grid, the electrical infrastructure may require a somewhat lesser degree of
vigilance than nuclear power plants or toxic chemical plants. Protection
should be concentrated on the largest, most critical plants and nodes in the
national system, especially ones that lack adequate redundant systems, perhaps several dozen nationwide. It might cost a few hundred million dollars
a year at most to protect these crucial systems.

The water supply is another serious concern because of possible chemical contamination, although the substantial amounts of chemicals needed

to contaminate a major water source would be quite difficult to deliver.[19] Terrorists could attack the water supply in other ways. They could lower water pressure, for example, by disabling pumps or electric power sources and thereby make it difficult to fight fires. But the effects would be less catastrophic than if lethal quantities of poison were introduced into a reservoir. To improve the security of the water supply, the relevant agencies should expand biological and chemical detectors in water reservoirs and pipes, and physically guard water reservoirs and critical pumps. In addition, water companies need to monitor their networks for signs that terrorists are using "backflow" to suck water into a home, contaminate it, and then send it back out to pipes that would carry it to other homes.[20] But a sense of proportion is in order here. Even though U.S. water treatment plants, along with nuclear facilities and national landmarks, have been mentioned in al-Qaida papers confiscated in Afghanistan, an attack on the water supply is likely to cause only moderate harm, given the difficulty of contaminating large amounts of water.[21] Thus on a scale of protection with toxic and nuclear plants at one extreme and most electricity infrastructure toward the other, the appropriate level of vigilance would probably fall somewhere in between. Annual expenses would be a few hundred million dollars nationwide, not the billions needed for more critical or potentially dangerous infrastructure.

Another crucial piece of the nation's infrastructure is the postal system. Not only could the system be disrupted under an attack, but it could also be used to deliver biological weapons, as demonstrated by the recent anthrax letters. Irradiating all mail is one option but would be costly both in terms of equipment and the extra time required for mail delivery. Radiation machines cost about $5 million. Chlorine dioxide gas chambers are cheaper but are still being tested.[22] The postal system's mail security plan would sanitize mail from public collection boxes at 290 major sorting centers, leaving close to 200 with no decontamination technology. At sorting centers without irradiation machines, improvements in the ventilation system and frequent vacuuming could reduce the risk of cross-contamination if a letter containing a harmful biological agent passed through the system. The postal system estimates its costs to combat bioterrorism will exceed $3 billion, some of which will be one-time costs; another $1 billion might be prudent for the sorting centers lacking decontamination technology plans.

Food safety, another challenge, is currently overseen by twelve agencies and addressed by as many as 35 statutes.[23] The Food Safety and Inspection Service (FSIS) in the Department of Agriculture inspects meat, poultry, and eggs, while the Food and Drug Administration (FDA) is responsible for inspecting most other foods. The resources and authority of these organizations vary. FSIS must certify that a country's food safety system meets U.S. standards for imported meat and poultry, and imports of food must remain in FSIS-registered warehouses until the FSIS approves their release. The FDA, however, has no legal authority to require a foreign country's food safety system to meet certain standards for exporting to the United States and does not control imported food when it arrives here. Therefore, the FDA must rely on inspections to identify unsafe food. Only 158 FDA inspectors monitored imported food in 2001.[24] With these limited resources, only 1 percent of food shipments into the United States were inspected.

Hiring additional food inspectors would make the food supply safer. The Bush administration has requested $46 million a year for hiring 412 inspectors, including 210 import inspectors, 100 domestic inspectors, and 100 inspectors who work in labs.[25] That might allow 5 to 10 percent of food to be inspected. Inspections of foreign producers should be substantially stepped up as well.[26] The costs associated with such inspections should be recovered through fees paid by the food companies.

A more fundamental reform to the food safety system appears necessary, however, particularly in the area of food inspections. These are still primarily physical (or "organoleptic") inspections, which were designed to meet basic public health requirements but are unlikely to detect microbiological or chemical hazards. The food safety system needs to substantially expand testing for such hazards.[27] Furthermore, food inspections should be consolidated into a single, independent agency with sufficient authority to safeguard the food supply. The General Accounting Office has endorsed such reforms, but congressional attempts to reorganize and strengthen food inspection have thus far met with industry resistance.[28] A consolidated agency may well decide to reduce the number of allowable entry points for food imports, as is already done by the Department of Agriculture. Finally, more stringent regulations for food producers, distributors, and importers—and larger fines for firms that violate the regulations—could make the food supply safer. Conducting background checks for certain employees, transporting food in more secure containers, and other measures could help prevent food tampering. The Department of Health and Human Services has issued voluntary regulations to help the food industry protect the food supply. Associated costs might be in the low hundreds of millions of dollars a year but should be offset by fees charged to industry, which would be borne by all consumers.

Cybersecurity, Telecommunications, and the Global Positioning Satellite System

Cybersecurity in the United States still requires significant improvement. Sharing information about threats is one means of protecting the critical components of the nation's telecommunications system against vulnerabilities. Currently, several industry groups share information on cyber threats among companies within the industry, but efforts at national information sharing have not been as successful (the government's Y2K clearinghouse being an exception).[29] Presidential Decision Directive 63 created the National Infrastructure Protection Center (NIPC) within the Department of Justice to serve as an information clearinghouse between the government and private sector. But the NIPC has not been adequately effective.

The government can take several steps to encourage better information sharing. First, all voluntarily shared information should be exempted from the Freedom of Information Act (FOIA), and all disseminated information should lack identification of its source. Second, authorities need to reconsider whether the NIPC should be located within the Justice Department. Although the Justice Department has competencies in cybersecurity, its law enforcement function makes private industry reluctant to share certain information. Third, the central clearinghouse should assume responsibility for mapping network interdependencies and testing information security systems throughout the nation, as proposed by the Hart-Rudman Commission on National Security/21st Century. The government should also share intelligence on cyber threats with other countries and coordinate procedures for investigating international cyber attacks. Finally, to ensure the sharing of the most important information, the government should consider mandating the reporting of security breaches that could threaten critical societal functions.

A second priority is to improve cybersecurity in the government's own information technology systems, including the networks that store and share nonclassified information.[30] These measures would have a dual purpose: they would protect important government information and provide an example to the private sector of best practices for computer security. According to one industry group, the federal government would need to spend $2.5 billion to protect its computer systems.[31] The government also needs to employ a sufficient number of skilled information technology professionals to protect its systems. Its salaries, work environment, and expectations regarding length of service must better adapt to the information technology labor market. The government could offer loan forgiveness and other incentives to recent college graduates with computer expertise who join the civil service; it could also expand the attractiveness of the so-called Senior-Level (SL) and Scientific or Professional (ST) positions within the civil service.[32] A more controversial government cybersecurity issue involves GovNet, a potentially more secure network exclusively for government use. GovNet would be a government-only Intranet, intended to be immune to outside viruses and attacks. But many cyberexperts are critical of the idea, arguing that any funds for GovNet would be better spent protecting the government's existing information technology assets.[33] The Bush administration has proposed a modest amount of funding for a GovNet feasibility study, and that approach—examining the feasibility of the idea rather than making a final decision on the initiative—seems prudent at this time.

Third, the government should increase funding for research and development on cybersecurity products. From a longer-term view, the government should take measures to increase domestic expertise in information technology and computer security. It could provide college scholarships for students with certain majors and promote the recruitment and professional development of math and science teachers at the K–12 levels (this type of effort is also needed for biological security).

Fourth, cybersecurity at private firms could benefit from stronger government regulations, especially for firms that provide critical societal functions. For example, they could be required to undertake regular "red team" exercises on their cyber vulnerabilities. In addition, as the National Research Council has noted, the government could encourage market incentives for better security, for example, by requiring insurance with varying premiums, depending on the quality of the firm's computer security and backup systems.[34]

The nation's telecommunications system plays a central role in the economy and in emergency response capabilities. In most major metropolitan areas, however, the fiber linkages that are central to both voice and data communications have inadequate backup systems. "Telecommunications hotels," which contain specialized switching and routing equipment and interconnect major fiber-optic cables, are geographically concentrated and may be insufficiently protected against physical attack.[35] The router software that is crucial to the Internet could also be hacked, and the Global Positioning Satellite system could be jammed in certain places.

Physical security should be improved around major telecommunications facilities and servers. The domain name system and root servers that play a central role in the Internet must also be better protected, for example, by subjecting programmers with administrative access to key systems to more extensive background and security checks and perhaps by creating a redundant domain name system.

A related issue involves the Global Positioning Satellite system, which is gradually being integrated into both public sector emergency response systems and private sector telecommunications and electronic infrastructure. The GPS is particularly vulnerable to terrorist attack, because it relies on a low-power signal that can be corrupted.[36] Steps should therefore be taken to improve GPS security. In particular, defense and emergency response systems should have backups in case of GPS interruptions. Over time, new satellites should be deployed with stronger signals that are more resistant to jamming, though the urgency of doing so immediately can be debated.

Transportation System

The nation's transportation system is clearly vulnerable to terrorist attack, but it would be impossible to protect all of the system's components at reasonable cost. Policymakers must therefore focus on areas where an attack could claim thousands of victims (for example, major bridges) or that represent a major infrastructure item that would have a systemic economic impact and which could not easily be replaced in a timely fashion. Air, rail, and auto travel must all come under close scrutiny.

Most of the required steps to improve airport security were incorporated into the Aviation Security Act, which establishes the Transportation Security Administration in the Department of Transportation and contains measures to improve airport security, the screening of luggage and passengers, and security onboard airplanes. Under this act, airport screeners will be federal employees, and all screeners must pass a background check and an annual proficiency review. An armed law enforcement officer must also be present at each security checkpoint. The Congressional Budget Office (CBO) expects the costs of screeners' salaries, training, background checks, and armed security at checkpoints to total about $4.5 billion over the period 2002–05.

The federal government must also purchase equipment to improve screening of carry-on luggage and to meet the new requirement that all checked luggage be screened.[37] A large investment in screening will be required, since only 165 screening machines currently exist.[38] The CBO estimates that the federal government will add 150 of these $1 million machines a year; the total cost for equipment purchases from 2002 to 2004 will be $600 million.[39] More may be needed, however, especially at smaller airports: these costs may then double.

The Aviation Security Act also adds federal law enforcement personnel to airports, air traffic facilities, and parked aircraft. The air marshal program will also place armed law enforcement agents on more flights. The aviation law requires air marshals on all flights that the secretary of transportation designates a high risk and states that long-distance nonstop flights should be a priority for the air marshal program. Assuming that 20 percent of all flights will have an air marshal on board, the total cost of the air marshal program and the airport facility security measures will be approximately $1 billion a year.

Finally, the Aviation Security Act strengthens regulations for airline security. It directs the FAA to issue regulations requiring airlines to strengthen and secure cockpit doors and prohibit any member of the flight crew not assigned to the flight deck from having a key to the door. Airlines must develop a security awareness program and provide an electronic passenger manifest, which includes visa and passport information, for every international flight entering the United States.

Additional security measures for the nation's rail system have already been proposed by Amtrak. They mainly consist of more law enforcement at stations, aboard trains, and at tunnels and bridges. Amtrak estimates annual costs of $61 million for increasing rail security.[40] It is doubtful that those costs are comprehensive, however. If one were concerned about making sure trains were not tampered with (say, by a terrorist placing a bomb in the undercarriage of a locomotive during off hours and setting it to go off when the train would be traveling at high speed near a populated area), more robust perimeter defenses would probably be needed. They could include, by analogy with Britain's efforts to counter the IRA, bomb shelter areas, much better lighting, closed-circuit TV monitoring, extensive fencing, and possibly ways to counter chemical or biological agents such as gas masks.[41]

Amtrak's requested funding for capital projects related to security and safety totals $454 million, $376 million of which is designated for system infrastructure security, including alarms, fencing and barriers, and lighting. Other items include a railroad incident command center, train locator and tracking, and remote engine cutoff. This capital spending would enhance railroad security, but some of it also addresses issues of rail safety unrelated to terrorist attacks. More may be needed, however.

Subway systems in major metropolitan areas could improve their resistance to terrorist attack by installing chemical detectors and other security devices, hiring more security guards for major stations and trains and regularly testing emergency plans. Washington, D.C., has recently begun activating chemical sensors in its Metro stations.[42] The Washington system, known as PROTECT, is expected to cost $81 million for all 47 underground stations, or just under $2 million per station. If similar ideas were adopted for the nation's other largest cities with subway systems, costs could reach close to $1 billion.[43]

Major bridges and tunnels are another concern, both because of the potential for mass human casualties and the economic and social disruption caused by any loss of these critical infrastructures. For bridges and tunnels over a threshold traffic volume, or at particularly key nodes in the transportation system, additional security precautions are needed. These can include tighter inspections before entry either at tolls or weigh stations, electronic monitoring of tunnels and bridges, and more police and security personnel at the site. In place of an outright restriction on trucks, the largest bridges and tunnels could allow only trusted shippers, subjected to additional security requirements, to have access, or they could introduce an EZ-pass system and require all trucks that do not qualify to be inspected. Such a system would reduce the greatest threat to bridges, tunnels, and truck cargoes, while still facilitating the timely transportation of crucial economic cargo. Also, capital improvements at crucial tunnels—including improved tunnel ventilation and evacuation routes—could help prevent or lessen the damage from an attack or accident. Annual costs would likely be in the hundreds of millions of dollars nationwide. For example, a sum of almost $1 billion has been proposed for fire safety improvements in river tunnels going into New York City to help speed up evacuations and rescue operations in case of a tunnel fire or a terrorist attack.[44]

Conclusion

This chapter has explored how to protect key targets within the United States from terrorist attack. Terrorists can shift their targets with such ease that special attention must be paid to this problem. In our view, policymakers should focus primarily on those targets at which an attack would involve large numbers of casualties, would entail significant economic costs, or would critically damage sites of high national significance. Although there is considerable overlap between our proposals and those of the Bush administration, we see a need for more resources in several areas, including cybersecurity, protection for chemical plants, food inspections, and protection for large buildings.

5

CONSEQUENCE
MANAGEMENT

This chapter takes up the fourth element of our homeland security concept—how the nation can mitigate the costs of a terrorist attack should one occur, also known as consequence management. Some progress has been made in preparing for chemical and conventional attacks under the Nunn-Lugar-Domenici program initiated in the mid-1990s, though more needs to be done in that arena as well. More recently, there has been a growing concern about responding to a biological attack. Table 5-1 presents the major areas of vulnerabilities and table 5-2 the options for addressing them. For the types of efforts considered here, Bush administration plans and budgets are generally quite similar to our own.

To begin, it is essential to know as soon as possible that an attack has occurred. In the case of biological attacks, that may not be easy. Ideally, major buildings, major intersections, subways, airports, and other places where crowds gather would be equipped with biological weapons detectors. Unfortunately, current technology does not permit economical production of small, effective detectors for biological agents.[1] The Bush administration wisely proposed to increase research and development

Table 5-1. *Managing the Consequences of Terrorist Attacks in the United States*

Area of vulnerability	Management needs
Training	Training of first responders Training of health professionals
Construction and capacity	Decontamination facilities Capacity for massive influx of hospital patients Stock of protective gear and medical supplies
Communications systems	Compatibility of communications systems Disease surveillance systems Communication between disaster relief and emergency organizations Backup communications systems within hospitals
Research and development	New vaccines and antibiotics New filters and detection systems

funding for such technologies, building on increases provided during the Clinton administration.[2]

But in the interval before good detectors capable of continuous monitoring for biological agents can be built, what should the nation do? The most promising approach depends on readiness at the local level. First responders will inevitably be drawn primarily from local fire and police departments, and local health facilities, which must be able to cope with the immediate aftereffects of an attack and communicate with national authorities in a timely fashion.[3]

Consequence management can be organized into four broad categories: training, construction and capacity, communication systems, and research and development. The first category includes field exercises alongside medical, safety, and administrative training. The second category includes the physical infrastructure and equipment inventory, as well as the personnel, needed to successfully respond to a terrorist attack. The third category encompasses improvements in all levels of communication, from supporting medical care providers to maintaining an informed public. The fourth category involves research and development that could, in the longer run,

Table 5-2. *Options to Improve Consequence Management*

Area of concern	Specific measure	Approximate annual cost[a] (billions of dollars)
Preferred options		
Training and research	Expand Nunn-Lugar-Domenici program[b]	1.0
	Improve training of medical personnel in recognizing symptoms of biological attack[b]	0.1
Construction and capacity	Stockpile more antibiotics and vaccines both nationally and locally[b]	0.5
	Make at least one hospital per region capable of handling victims of contagious biological attack[b]	0.3
Communication and information systems	Construct electronic network at home and abroad for syndrome surveillance	0.3
	Construct international network for syndrome surveillance, help fund efforts of poorer countries	0.3
	Purchase dependable communications gear linking hospitals, fire and police, and national authorities for emergencies[b]	0.2
Research and development	Expand development of antibiotics, vaccines, other medications[b]	0.5
	Total low/modest cost	3.1[c]
Higher-cost/least-risk further options	Make every hospital capable of handling victims of contagious biological attack	1.0
	Expand hospital bed capacity	5.0
	Buy individual protective gear for all citizens	3.0
	Purchase audiovisual and computer capabilities for remote diagnosis	0.5

a. Annual cost relative to original pre-9/11 2002 budget.

b. Denotes similar initiative of comparable magnitude proposed by the Bush administration.

c. Detail may not sum to total because of rounding.

dramatically improve the nation's ability to contain specific types of terrorist attacks (see table 5-2 for specifics).

Training

The Nunn-Lugar-Domenici program, created to help cities deal with large-scale terrorism, provides training to local police departments, fire departments, and hospitals in large cities for responding to an attack, particularly with conventional or chemical weapons. The program has unfortunately not fulfilled its potential. For one thing, its many emergency response teams and training courses are run mainly by military offices—such as the Army's Domestic Preparedness Program, National Guard Civil Support teams, Marine Corps chemical rescue team, and the Air Force Prime BEEF units. However, the military would be unlikely to provide the first responders in a no-notice domestic attack, since its units would probably not be on the scene right away.[4] For another, the various training programs are not well coordinated; redundancies are common. Many of the courses teach little new material, and health care providers do not regularly attend.[5]

One type of training that should be expanded is field exercises to test federal, state, and local coordinated emergency response systems. Previous exercises, such as "TOPOFF 2000," have proved helpful in identifying shortcomings and communication failures. Future training exercises should extend to the local level and include more hospital facilities. Hospitals should also conduct their own exercises more regularly. Under Joint Commission on Accreditation of Healthcare Organizations (JCAHO) standards, hospitals are required to run through their own individual emergency plans twice a year, either in response to a real emergency or as a drill.[6] Unfortunately, many of these plans are not designed to deal with all aspects of biological, chemical, radiological, nuclear, or conventional disasters.[7]

First-responder training, also a high priority, could be improved by expanding the Nunn-Lugar-Domenici program. Follow-up training needs to become more regular and rigorous, standards for protective equipment should be raised, and more cities should be brought into the effort. So far, funding has averaged about $40 million a year, but it should be increased to at least $1 billion a year (as the administration now intends).[8]

Another pressing imperative is to improve the ability of the health system to recognize and contain biological and chemical attacks. Early recognition of and intervention in a biological attack would substantially reduce the casualties and costs involved.[9] The health industry can help improve its ability to recognize and contain a biological or chemical attack through medical training. Clinical staff and lab technicians should become familiar with symptoms and pathogens of bioterrorism so they can more quickly diagnose infectious diseases, know how they are transmitted, and determine the proper treatment.[10] Such training will help avoid unnecessary contamination of the staff themselves, other patients, and medical facilities. Current medical competency in these areas is woefully low; one recent report demonstrated substantial shortcomings in identifying inhalation anthrax at a prominent hospital, and other reports have documented similar deficiencies more broadly.[11] Instruments and tests for detection and identification of chemical or biological agents or radiation could also be used to quickly determine causes of illness.[12]

The health sector requires safety training as well. Staff and medical personnel should be able to identify and react calmly to a terrorist attack, even a hoax like a bomb threat. They should be familiar with decontamination procedures with either hazardous materials or infectious patients.[13] They should know how to locate and use decontamination facilities and personal protective equipment (PPE), such as gowns, masks, gloves, boots, and respiratory protective equipment, if needed.

Administrative training is also important. Staff at hospitals should be comfortable with triage procedures for a large influx of patients and know how to prioritize their need for care and track them through the system. For mass casualty disasters, plans to distribute victims among other health care providers should be prearranged.[14] Hospital personnel should also understand crowd control techniques: how to separate media from victims, for example, and how to credential volunteers.[15] In the long run, training in the foregoing areas could be best achieved and maintained through standards developed and institutionalized in local and state training academies, as well as in nursing and medical schools.

Construction and Capacity

The health system needs a larger physical infrastructure, equipment inventory, and manpower if it is to handle emergencies caused by a terrorist attack appropriately. For contagious diseases (those that can be passed from person to person), in particular, it is important to be able to isolate infected patients. At least one hospital in any given region should therefore have a quarantine-like environment in which such victims could be admitted and treated. Decontamination units need to be in place outside the hospital, or at least there should be a plan for how to separate patients with contagious diseases and decontaminate them.

Currently, there is no standard requiring hospitals to maintain a decontamination unit, and few have one.[16] Hence contamination by just a small number of patients can lead hospitals to close down.[17] To avoid such closings, the JCAHO recommends (but does not mandate) that hospitals' emergency management plans include preparations for decontamination areas.[18] The American Hospital Association calls for at least some sort of decontamination facility on site with plans for overload, whether through access to a regional facility or the use of portable outdoor units.[19] At the very least, new hospitals being built and those under renovation should be required to include decontamination showers and compartmentalized ventilation systems to better prepare for infectious situations.[20]

Hospitals must also have the resources to expand bed capacity; increase the number of available clinical staff; stockpile antibiotics, vaccines, and medical supplies; and be prepared to increase their morgue capacities. In addition, hospitals must have backup plans to provide for overload in any of these areas before an emergency occurs.[21]

For larger-scale emergencies, hospital bed capacity could be a problem. Hospital staff must know how many beds will be available in a crisis and be able to expand treatment areas when needed.[22] The trend in the health care sector, however, is to reduce capacity, so hospitals would be less able to handle a mass influx of patients.[23] Some have even turned away new patients when filled to capacity with influenza cases.[24] The Veterans Administration (VA) hospital system is supposed to serve as a backup facility to communities experiencing major disasters, but the number of beds it maintains has also declined significantly in recent years.[25] Given the extremely high cost of maintaining excess bed capacity, only a higher-end and higher-cost approach to homeland security would try to expand such capacity in a significant way. Other options might be to identify locations where basic medical care could be provided in emergencies (such as hotels, "tent" hospitals, or other facilities) and to develop plans for releasing certain categories of less-ill patients to free up more hospital beds in a crisis.

Along with more beds and nurses, hospitals need an adequate stock of protective gear, as well as at least a 24-hour supply of antibiotics, vaccines, medical supplies, and surgical equipment.[26] The VA maintains a national stockpile of pharmaceutical supplies (the National Pharmaceutical Stockpile) that is supposed to be transportable anywhere in the country within 12 hours of deployment, and a larger stockpile is available within 24 to 36 hours through a vendor-managed arrangement.[27] Still, readily accessible amounts need to be immediately available on site in an emergency situation. Stockpiles could be maintained on a regional level, with health care facilities rotating the supply through regular use to avoid expiration.[28] Enough respiratory protective equipment, ventilators, and other extra surgical and general medical supplies (patient linens, hospital scrubs) should also be available to operate an emergency department during the onset of a disaster until replacement supplies arrive. Some hospitals have made arrangements to have vendors automatically send regular shipments of supplies during an emergency.[29]

A more difficult issue includes vaccination. The administration has proposed rings of quarantines, but it is unclear whether quarantine would be effective. Because universal vaccination is also risky, the trade-off is a difficult one and merits debate.

The fear of biological (or chemical) attacks may lead some to propose acquiring protective gear for each citizen. Costs could range from $100 to $300 or more per person, for a national cost of $30 billion or more. Such expenditures seem unnecessary, however, given the small probability that people would have such equipment nearby during an attack and the fact that other, more economical types of protection against biological and chemical attack are available (which would protect key buildings and other gathering points). But a hypothetical high-end program might include personal equipment.[30] The government might also provide information for citizens on where such equipment can be purchased, should they want it.

Communication and Information Systems

The third category of consequence management entails communication. During a disaster, communication is essential to the coordination of relief efforts and the flow of information—both of which are necessary to keep emergency response systems functional and reduce stress and panic. Lines of communication need to be in place nationwide so that first responders can talk with one another, specialized teams can communicate with the first responders, appropriate people and supplies can be sent to the scene of a disaster as quickly as possible, and accurate information about the circumstances can be relayed to the responders. Regionally and locally, health care providers need a community-based response system that can deal with the full range of diseases and disasters. Internally, hospitals need backup communication systems in case main lines are unavailable.

First responders for possible conventional, chemical, and other such attacks also need dependable communications systems, possibly including priority access to wireless networks (as long as they do not dominate them). The Bush administration has recommended just such a capability in its 2003 budget.[31]

A disease surveillance system at some wide-reaching level is an essential tool both before and after a disaster or epidemic occurs. Once an epidemic was discovered, such a system would streamline communication about the situation among states and public health officials.[32] It could also include connections to information on available antibiotics and vaccines and help mobilize resources for their deployment. This surveillance should be supplemented by a widespread lab diagnostic system that would provide a nationally accessible database of diseases with their symptoms, dangerous effects, and treatments, when available.

Funding for tracking infectious disease and carrying out "syndrome surveillance" worldwide is also needed. By analogy with the costs of other large information technology networks, the total amount here could reach several billion dollars—which is far beyond the $300 million initially appropriated for local hospitals and health departments in the immediate aftermath of September 11 ($60 million of which was for food inspections, an important and related, but still largely separate, task).[33]

Regionally and locally, hospitals must establish relationships with other health care providers and voluntary disaster relief organizations so as to be able to call on them for additional support. Relationships with police and fire departments will also be important, to provide hospital security and decontamination help respectively. A community network could be organized to post information required to coordinate all these efforts.[34] All the measures just discussed are crucial ingredients of an effective community emergency response system. This system must focus not only on responses at the disaster site, but also on the whole process of treatment and recovery.

Internally, hospitals need to have alternate communication systems in place in case of a system failure or overload. These may include multiple phone lines; a computer with Intranet, Internet, and e-mail capabilities; web-based video-conferencing; two-way radios; and a copy machine, ham radio, cell phones, pagers, broadcast fax machines, loudspeakers, bullhorns, and even human couriers.[35] A central command center will be needed to disseminate all important information to both staff and the media.[36] Equally important, clear signage plans for directing staff, volunteers, families and friends of victims, media, or anyone else in the hospital must be in place to avoid confusion and the disruption of medical care services.[37] Hospitals must also be able to keep track of their patients. Patient-tracking systems and translators for non-English-speaking patients will be key to achieving that result.[38]

Research and Development

For maximum effectiveness, consequence management needs input from research and development, not only in the way of new vaccines and antibiotics but also information about newly discovered or newly recurring infectious diseases and treatments for chemical and radiological terrorism. Furthermore, researchers should explore methods for strengthening the human body's immune system, an objective that some biologists believe may be within reach because of the promising results of preliminary experiments.[39]

The cost of bringing a single new drug to market is often half a billion dollars, and a number of new drugs will be needed in the years ahead. For these reasons, it seems useful to add $500 million a year to the current National Institutes of Health budget on bioterrorism, currently about $100 million.[40] It may also be necessary to provide liability protections to manufacturers in order to encourage sufficient supplies of antibiotics and vaccines.

Emergency response equipment to deal with contamination should also be developed.[41] R&D efforts should also be directed at improving chemical and biological detection equipment. Biological detectors available today are neither cheap nor small nor fast; they should be all three but cannot reach these levels without a substantial investment of time, work, and money.

Conclusion

Consequence management efforts to date have focused largely on possible attacks more likely to involve chemical or conventional weapons than biological ones. These types of attacks vary considerably as to when they would be noticed, whom they would afflict, and how they would have to be treated. For these reasons, the Bush administration's decisions to focus on biological terrorism and on the needs of local responders for better gear, communications equipment, and training are prudent. Our proposals are quite similar to the administration's proposals in these areas, though we do see a need for greater investment in public health information technologies and certain other specific areas.

6

Principles for Providing and Financing Homeland Security

Now that we have outlined a specific homeland security agenda, the next question to address is who should implement and pay for the proposed measures? The basic issue here is which measures should be the responsibility of the federal, state, and local governments, on one hand, and the private sector, on the other. We provide some broad principles in this regard but emphasize that specific policy responses depend on the sector and institutional setting (see chapters 2–5 for the policy steps relevant in each setting).

Assigning responsibility for homeland security, as in other areas, can be problematic because the desire to be fair may be inconsistent with the desire to provide sound incentives. For example, federal financing of private sector antiterrorism measures may strike some Americans as fair but could also lead policymakers to adopt unnecessarily expensive measures. At the same time, some forms of federal financing could strike Americans as unfair but could play a crucial role in encouraging appropriate levels of investment in security. Policymakers must therefore strike a balance between fairness and cost-effectiveness, and the balance will likely vary from sector to sector. Moreover, given the uncertainties involved and the constantly changing nature of the potential threat, policymakers are best advised to experiment with alternative approaches and to learn incrementally from experience. Flexibility, especially as new risks manifest themselves and experience accumulates, is likely to be essential to an effective response to terrorism.

Nonetheless, the nation must start somewhere, and we suggest several principles for guiding the initial steps in the four general areas described in the preceding chapters: minimizing terrorist access to the country, tracking terrorists and limiting access to dangerous materials within the country, protecting key sites and activities within the United States, and reducing the toll from any attacks that do occur. As mentioned earlier in this volume, minimizing terrorist access to the country and reducing the costs of any attacks that do occur are primarily governmental functions, as is the tracking of potential terrorists domestically.[1] The principal questions with respect to these categories, therefore, are what level of government should undertake the measures and whether that same level of government should finance them.

Some of the thorniest issues, however, revolve around preventive activities and the protection of key sites within the United States. Inhibiting access to dangerous materials and protecting domestic sites, in particular, raise difficult questions. Why should the government be involved in protecting private property and activities within the United States against terrorist attacks, how should it be involved, and who should pay for the required security measures?

These are all complex issues, but we stress two points in this chapter: (1) some government action is necessary in order to provide appropriate protection against terrorist attacks on private property within the United States, and (2) the various users, providers, and owners of the property or activity should generally pay for the costs associated with the additional security. Furthermore, in most cases, the action should take the form of performance-oriented mandates on the private sector, perhaps coupled with insurance requirements or incentives, rather than direct subsidies or tax incentives. This approach, although imperfect, best balances the various trade-offs currently facing policymakers in designing cost-effective and equitable protection against terrorist threats in private sector settings. As explained later in the chapter, the purpose of the "stakeholder-pays" approach is to discourage activity in the most dangerous settings, ensure that security measures are not gold-plated, discourage excessive rent seeking (that is, an intense pursuit of excess profits through government protection or other means), and promote innovation in antiterrorism security.

We also suggest how to implement and finance antiterrorism steps in public institutions, such as public hospitals or the local police force. In our opinion, the federal government should finance those steps that specifically and primarily address terrorist threats. But state and local governments should finance any such measures that carry substantial benefits within their own jurisdictions (in addition to affecting their ability to prevent or address terrorist attacks). The larger the local benefit of a specific measure in relation to the antiterrorism benefit, the larger the local and state share of the costs should be. Thus the federal government should finance specialized antiterrorism training and equipment for police and fire departments, but it should not finance the hiring of additional police or firefighters.

An Efficient Response to Terrorist Threats in the Private Sector

This section examines antiterrorism measures in largely private sector settings, such as commercial buildings, athletic arenas, or commercial travel. Government policies toward such measures should reflect several offsetting considerations, including the "external" effects terrorist acts create beyond the impacts on their immediate targets, the need to avoid excessive costs in achieving any given level of protection against terrorism, the potential for innovation in providing security, and the fairness of different approaches.

Externalities, Market Failures, and the Need for Government Intervention

The first question that arises here is why government intervention is needed at all. Indeed, a top official at the Environmental Protection Agency recently argued that a federal counterterrorism security standard for chemical plants or refineries may be unnecessary because the "industry has a very powerful incentive to do the right thing. It ought to be their worst nightmare that their facility would be a target of a terrorist act because they did not meet their responsibility to their community."[2] Individuals and corporations do indeed have powerful incentives to protect themselves against terrorist attacks.[3] But why is that *private* motivation not sufficient to provide an optimal amount of protection for *society* as whole?

There are at least six potential justifications for government intervention.

First, security against terrorism involves a negative externality. For example, loose security at a chemical facility can provide terrorists with the materials they need for an attack. Similarly, poor security at a biological laboratory can provide terrorists with access to dangerous pathogens. The costs that follow from allowing terrorists to obtain access to such materials and successfully carry out attacks are generally not borne by the facilities themselves. Such a negative externality provides a compelling rationale for government intervention to protect highly explosive materials, chemicals, and biological pathogens even if they are stored in private facilities.[4] More broadly, a negative externality can arise wherever the security of one firm is adversely affected by poor security at another firm. In the presence of such negative externalities, private markets will undertake less investment in security than would be socially desirable. Individuals or firms deciding how best to protect themselves against terrorism are unlikely to take the external costs of an attack fully into account and therefore will generally provide an inefficiently low level of security against terrorism on their own.[5] Without government involvement, private markets will thus typically underinvest in antiterrorism measures.[6]

Second, a significant terrorist attack not only causes material damage, but also undermines the nation's sovereignty by exposing our vulnerability. It may also embolden other terrorists or adversaries, and hinder our ability to carry out an intended agenda. In this case, the associated costs may be difficult to quantify, but are nonetheless real. In other words, the costs of a terrorist act extend well beyond the immediate areas and people affected to the entire nation.

Third, government intervention can be justified by the cost and difficulty of accurately evaluating security measures. One reason that governments promulgate building codes, for example, is that it would be too difficult for each individual to evaluate a building's structural soundness before deciding whether to enter it. Since it would also be difficult for the individual to evaluate how well the building's air intake system could filter out potential bioterrorist attacks, the same logic could suggest that the government should set minimum antiterrorism standards for buildings if there were a nontrivial threat of a terrorist attack on the relevant type of building (so that the individual would have some interest in ensuring that the building was protected against biological attack). Similarly, it would be possible, but inefficient, for each individual to conduct extensive biological antiterrorism safety tests on the food that he or she was about to consume. The information costs associated with that type of system, however, make it much less attractive than a system of government regulation of food safety.

Fourth, corporate and individual financial exposure to the losses from a major terrorist attack are inherently limited by the bankruptcy laws. To illustrate, assume that there are two types of possible terrorist attacks on a specific firm: a very severe attack and a somewhat more modest one. Under either type of attack, the losses imposed would exceed the firm's net assets, the firm would declare bankruptcy, and therefore the extent of the losses beyond that which would bankrupt the firm would be irrelevant to the firm's owners. Since the outcome for the firm's owners would not depend on the severity of the attack, the firm would have little or no incentive to reduce the likelihood of the more severe version of the attack even if the required preventive steps were relatively inexpensive. From society's perspective, however, such security measures may be beneficial, and government intervention can therefore be justified to address catastrophic possibilities in the presence of the bankruptcy laws.

Fifth, the private sector may expect the government to bail it out should a terrorist attack occur. (The financial assistance to the airline industry provided by the government following the September 11 attacks provides just one example of such bailouts.) Such expectations create a moral hazard problem: they lead private firms to neglect undertaking as much security as they otherwise would.[7] If the government cannot credibly convince the private sector that no bailouts will occur after an attack, it may have to intervene before an attack to offset the adverse incentives created by the expectation of a bailout.

Sixth, government intervention may be necessary in the face of incomplete markets. The most relevant examples involve imperfections in capital and insurance markets. In the latter case, if insurance firms are unable to obtain reinsurance coverage for terrorism risks (that is, if primary insurers are not able to transfer some of the risk from terrorism costs to other insurance firms in the reinsurance market), some government involvement may be warranted. In addition, certain types of activities may require large-scale coordination, which may be possible but difficult to achieve without governmental intervention.

The importance of these six factors varies from situation to situation. Furthermore, the benefits of government intervention must be weighed against the costs of government failure, where the government intervention may do more harm than good. Even if an omniscient government could theoretically improve homeland security in a manner that provides larger benefits than costs, it is not clear that real-world governments (suffering from political pressures, imperfect information, and skewed bureaucratic incentives) would do so. Furthermore, the potential for government failure depends on the characteristics of the government agency and the sector involved. For example, it seems plausible that government failure is a particular danger in innovative and rapidly evolving markets.[8]

Both the need for government intervention and the potential costs associated with it thus vary from sector to sector, as should the policy response. But in general, it seems that we cannot just "leave it up to the market" in protecting ourselves against terrorist threats. The market has an important role to play, but government intervention in some form and in some markets will be necessary to fashion the appropriate response to terrorism.

Judging Measures to Reduce the Costs of Terrorism

The need for some sort of government action to provide appropriate protection for private property and individuals against terrorism does not define how or in which situations the government should intervene. The various tools that the government could employ, furthermore, will likely determine how costly the intervention will be, as well as who will bear those costs. For example, to improve safety in commercial buildings, the government could

—*Impose direct regulation.* The federal government could require that certain antiterrorist features be included in any commercial or public building.[9]

—*Require insurance.* The federal government could require every commercial or public building to carry insurance against terrorism (much as state governments now typically require motorists to carry some form of auto liability insurance).[10] The logic of such a requirement is that insurance companies would then provide incentives for buildings to be safer.

—*Provide a subsidy for antiterrorism activities.* The federal government could provide a subsidy—through direct government spending or through a tax incentive—for investing in antiterrorism building features or for other steps to protect buildings against attacks.

More broadly, each of the various approaches for minimizing the dangers and damages related to terrorism likely entails a different level of aggregate costs, and also a different distribution of those costs across sectors and individuals.[11] Cost-effectiveness is important because it reduces the economic burden of achieving any given level of security (see box 6-1).

The traditional approach to evaluating the various governmental approaches to improving homeland security would involve cost-benefit analysis, under which the costs and benefits of the various approaches would be compared and the one with the largest net benefits would be favored. In the terrorism context, however, the value of traditional cost-benefit analysis is not obvious. For example, given our current state of knowledge, it does not appear to be possible to determine with precision the quantitative benefits of any given tool, that is, to determine by precisely how much it reduces the risk of any potential terrorist attack (or the extent to which the action limits the damages any attack may cause).[12]

How then, should, policymakers decide which of these tools is more appropriate in any given situation? Realizing the difficulty of the task, we suggest that the applicability of any particular policy to any particular type of terrorist risk in private sector settings be judged according to at least the following (somewhat related) criteria. The criteria highlight the importance of incentives, which are central to fashioning cost-effective government intervention in the private sector, and fairness:

—To what degree would the tool affect private behavior?

—To what degree would the change in private behavior reduce the overall risk from terrorist activity, as opposed to merely shift it from one venue to another?

—How well will the government make decisions in this area, and how well will it avoid imposing unnecessary costs?

—How fair is the expected outcome? Will society accept the consequences in terms of income or wealth distribution?

Box 6-1. *The Economic Impact of the Homeland Security Effort and Terrorist Attacks*

The measures we propose in previous chapters would involve federal costs of roughly $45 billion a year and up to $10 billion in private-sector costs.

These increased security efforts will reduce measured economic output, because they will displace both capital and labor from activities that would produce final goods and services. Improved security is not recorded in the national accounts, so spending $1 on equipment that improves security rather than $1 on equipment that makes goods will ultimately reduce measured economic activity. In other words, because we will be investing more in security, we will be investing less in other productive capital, while also diverting workers from activities that raise measured output and into security-related activities. (Note that insurance premiums should generally be counted as a cost of the homeland security effort only to the extent that they are not actuarially fair; actuarially fair premiums represent a transfer of resources, not an overall resource cost.)

The homeland security effort could reduce both the level of output and its growth rate over time. For example, delays in the transportation system associated with improved security and the initial diversion of both labor and capital into security activities could reduce real output levels by between 0.3 and 0.5 percentage points. But to the extent that providing a given level of security requires a growing share of inputs over time, the effort would also reduce productivity growth rates over time. Evidence from capital expenditures on pollution abatement equipment, which peaked at the equivalent of more than $100 billion per year, suggests that the homeland security effort may reduce measured real growth rates by 0.1 percentage point or less per year.

Careful design of government regulations and scrutiny of the government's own spending on homeland security to ensure its cost-effectiveness can reduce the economic burden of achieving homeland security. Given the national income accounting system, government expenditures on homeland security will contribute to measured GDP. Nonetheless, such expenditures may still produce indirect economic costs and lower levels of productivity relative to what would have otherwise occurred (either by crowding out more productive government expenditures or by reducing national saving). That is precisely why the principles delineated in this chapter and the more detailed recommendations made in previous chapters are intended to produce a cost-effective approach to homeland security. (It is worth noting in this regard that the government does not currently track security spending by private firms. Given the increased importance associated with security measures, it is important to know how much is being spent on such activities. The Bureau of Economic Analysis, within the Department of Commerce, should create a supplemental account to the National Income and Product Accounts to track such spending.)

Such costs must be weighed against the costs of the terrorist attacks they help to prevent. The September 11 attack, for example, imposed economic costs of perhaps $100 billion or so. Other attacks could prove even more costly if they involved larger losses of life or more prolonged interruptions to economic activity.

Examining the costs of September 11 in more detail may be illuminating as a guide to the benefits of an effective homeland security strategy. The costs from the terrorist attacks have two main components: the direct loss of physical and human capital as a result of the attack, and the macroeconomic costs caused by the interruption to normal business activities. (Note that a small component of the macroeconomic loss reflects the loss in physical and human capital from the attack, so that there is a small element of double counting in this approach.)

Current estimates suggest that insured losses from the attacks—which provide a proxy for the direct loss of physical and human capital—may amount to between $36 billion and $54 billion. The macroeconomic cost from interrupting business activities following the attacks is more difficult to measure, since many factors influence the behavior of the macroeconomy and since some of the reduction in activity in September caused by the attacks may merely have been shifted into later months. It is possible to put a plausible upper bound on the potential effect, however.

In particular, on September 10, 2001, the Blue Chip consensus estimate for real GDP growth in the third quarter of 2001 was 1.6 percent (on a seasonally adjusted, annualized basis). The consensus estimate for real GDP growth in the fourth quarter was 2.6 percent. In the aftermath of the attack, which occurred in the final month of the third quarter, the real GDP growth figures turned out to be −1.3 percent in the third quarter and 1.7 percent in the fourth quarter. Even if the entire difference between the Blue Chip estimate and the actual outcome is attributed to the September 11 attacks, and even if we assume that none of the reduction in activity at the end of 2001 is subsequently offset by increased activity in 2002, the cost of the lost production amounts to about $100 billion.

A more reasonable but still generous figure assumes that, say, half of the reduction in economic activity during the third and fourth quarters is either unrelated to the attacks or will be offset by increased activity in the future. In that case, the loss from reduced economic activity amounts to about $50 billion, and the direct loss to physical and human capital also amounts to about $50 billion. The total loss is then about $100 billion. Even this figure is likely to exaggerate the cost of the September 11 attacks, because it is unlikely that as much as half the reduction in economic activity during the third and fourth quarters was due to the attacks and would not be offset by higher activity later.

Effectiveness of Instruments of Government Intervention

With these criteria in mind, we now review briefly each of the instruments of government action described earlier and attempt, at least in a broad way (since some points have already been raised in previous chapters), to judge how effective they are likely to be.

Regulation

The principal benefit of a regulatory approach is that the regulatory standard provides a minimum guarantee regarding antiterrorism protection (assuming the regulations are enforced).[13] It also can discourage the most dangerous activities. If skyscrapers are natural targets for terrorists, requiring security measures in new skyscrapers discourages their construction (and also raises the cost of living in them, even if they are built), which may be an appropriate means of diminishing the nation's exposure to catastrophic attack, given the buildings' assumed attractiveness to terrorists.

But there are also downsides to regulation. First, the minimum regulatory threshold may be set at an inappropriate level.[14] Second, a regulatory approach, especially one that consists of "commands and controls" rather than market-like incentives, can be an unnecessarily expensive mechanism for achieving a given level of security.[15] Third, this approach does not generally provide incentives for innovation. Firms would be motivated to meet the minimum regulatory standard, but not necessarily exceed it. Indeed, depending on how they are written, rules may impede innovation in finding new (and less costly) approaches to improving protection against terrorism, especially if they are of the "command-and-control" variety.

These costs can be reduced, although not eliminated, through careful attention to the design of the regulations. In particular, the more that they focus on processes and performance, rather than specific inputs, the better. For example, a regulation affecting an indoor athletic arena could state that the arena's air ventilation system must be able to contain a given type of bioterrorist attack within a specific amount of time, rather than that the system must include specific devices. Compliance with the performance-based regulation could then be tested regularly by government inspectors. Such a system gives firms at least some incentive to design and implement less expensive mechanisms for achieving any given level of security.[16]

A final issue here is fairness. Regulation imposes its costs on the users and providers of a particular service. Such a "stakeholder-pays" approach may strike some Americans as unfair, especially since many of the stakeholders would have made physical and human capital investments before the threat of terrorism manifested itself in a significant manner.[17] But it may strike other Americans as eminently fair: from this perspective, those who engage in the most dangerous activities (in terms of their exposure to terrorist attacks) should pay for the costs associated with those risks. Furthermore, since higher earners likely represent a disproportionate share of the stakeholders in many of the most vulnerable services (such as air travel) and buildings (such as skyscrapers), the stakeholder-pays approach may also strike many Americans as equitable from an income inequality perspective.

Insurance Requirement

An insurance requirement is an alternative to direct government regulation.[18] At first glance, such a requirement may seem counterproductive. Firms and individuals who have insurance against terrorism would appear to lack incentives to take appropriate precautions against an attack. Where such insurance is available, however, it typically comes with provisions (such as deductibles, coinsurance, and coverage limits) to ensure that the insured bear at least some of the cost of an attack and thus have at least some economic incentive to avoid such attacks or minimize their consequences. Furthermore, the insurance companies themselves have an incentive to encourage risk-reducing activities.[19] Insurance firms could provide incentives for measures that reduce the exposure of buildings to terrorist attack (such as protecting or moving the air intake), or that reduce the likelihood of a successful cyberattack on a computer system or Intranet (such as improved firewalls and more advanced encryption).

Universal insurance is clearly not a panacea, however.[20] A particular concern is that the insurance premium market may not work that well in discriminating among terrorism risks. Indeed, the fairness of allowing differential premiums to discriminate among different exposures to terrorism is unclear. Consider the higher risks for such "iconic" structures as the World Trade Center, the Empire State Building, and other tall structures elsewhere in the country. If insurers are not restricted by government policy from charging appropriately risk-related premiums, insurance markets will discourage the construction of such potential terrorist targets in the future. Such an outcome may be efficient in the sense of reducing potential exposure to terrorist attacks, but socially undesirable in another if the buildings have substantial symbolic value.

Furthermore, allowing substantial variations in insurance premiums would impose costs on the owners of tall buildings. In evaluating the effects of such costs, a distinction should be drawn between existing buildings and new construction. The owners of existing buildings likely did not anticipate the terrorist threat when the buildings were constructed. Any additional costs on such existing buildings would reduce their market values, imposing capital losses on their owners. Some may not view this outcome as fair: it effectively imposes much higher costs on the owners (or occupants) of an existing building to address a threat that was largely unexpected when the buildings were constructed. Others may view the outcome as eminently fair, since the alternative would be to have the population as a whole effectively provide a subsidy to the owners of prominent buildings. Furthermore, failing to allow insurance firms to discriminate across risks in pricing policies could induce "cherry picking" of the lowest risks by the insurance firms and make it difficult for the higher risks to obtain the insurance from any firm. (In the United Kingdom, a government-sponsored mutual insurance organization, Pool Re, provides antiterrorism insurance. The rates vary by location, with the highest in Central London and the lowest in rural parts of Scotland and Wales.)[21] For new construction, the case for differentiated insurance premiums is stronger, since the prospective owners are now aware of the threat of attack and since differentiated premiums could play an important role in encouraging safer designs of prominent buildings.

In any event, even without government prohibition of risk-related premiums, if government regulators find it difficult to undertake comparative benefit analysis in fighting terrorism, private insurers would be highly likely to face similar challenges. The absence of solid actuarial information on the risks involved reflects the nation's good fortune thus far in not being exposed to a large number of terrorist attacks but makes it much more difficult for private insurers to price the risks associated with terrorism. So too does the fact that terrorists can shift their targets and respond to security measures in a manner that does not arise with regard to natural risks. Nonetheless, as the Congressional Budget Office has noted, "Not every new risk has proved to be uninsurable. For example, the changing legal environment for product liability, which makes predicting losses difficult, has affected how insurers manage such risks, but it has not resulted in insurers' dropping all product liability coverage. Rather it has produced a combination of more restricted coverage, shared responsibility, and modifications in producers' behavior." CBO also notes that private insurers in Israel provide some antiterrorism coverage (involving indirect losses such as the costs of business interruptions from terrorist attacks).[22]

Perhaps most fundamentally, an insurance system will not work if insurers do not offer the insurance (or offer it only at extremely high prices in relation to some underlying actuarial model). A particular concern involves reinsurance: the transfer of risk from the primary insurance company to another entity. Rather than maintaining high reserves to meet the potential costs of extreme events, primary insurance firms buy reinsurance from other firms. The reinsurance covers at least part of a severe loss, attenuating the risks faced by the primary insurers. Reinsurance firms, however, have generally stopped offering reinsurance on terrorism risks. In response, many primary insurance companies have eliminated terrorism coverage from their policies (when allowed by state commissioners to do so).[23]

Thus far, lenders appear to be providing credit to commercial borrowers who lack terrorism insurance.[24] But it is unclear how sustainable—or desirable—such an outcome is. Even in the absence of an insurance mandate, policymakers should therefore explore a variety of options to facilitate the provision of terrorism insurance.

One possibility is a federal reinsurance program. In late 2001, both the House and Senate considered legislation that would provide catastrophic terrorism reinsurance assistance to the insurance industry, although the approaches differed somewhat and the Senate did not hold a vote on its legislation.[25] If federal reinsurance is provided, it is important that the insurance companies themselves face some liability in the case of a terrorist attack, so that they have an incentive to encourage efficient behavior among those they insure.[26] Such incentives could be provided, as under the House and Senate legislation, through deductibles that apply before the government reinsurance is available.[27] But a substantial flaw in both bills is that neither would impose a fee for the federal reinsurance effort. A better approach would have the government share the risk, but also the premiums, from primary terrorism insurance.[28] Finally, any such federal reinsurance program should be temporary. Over time, as new approaches to spreading the financial risks associated with antiterrorism insurance develop, the need for any government reinsurance program could be reduced.[29]

Any move toward a broader system of antiterrorism insurance thus faces substantial obstacles. Some economists and market observers have raised important questions about whether capital market imperfections impede the ability of insurers to provide coverage against catastrophic risks, such as those involved in terrorist activities.[30] Despite these potential problems, it is plausible that a broader system of antiterrorism insurance could develop over the medium to long term and thereby play a crucial role in providing incentives to private sector firms to undertake additional security measures when such steps are warranted given the risk of a terrorist attack (at least as viewed by the insurance firm).

Subsidies for Antiterrorism Measures

Government action can also take the form of subsidies for antiterrorism measures undertaken by private actors.[31] Subsidies could affect firm behavior and (if appropriately designed) provide some protection against terrorist threats. Subsidies carry four dangers, however. First, they can encourage unnecessarily expensive investments in security measures (or "gold plating").[32] Second, they would likely prompt firms to engage in intensive lobbying to capture the subsidies, which would not only dissipate resources that could have been used more productively elsewhere, but may skew the definition of what qualifies for the subsidy toward inappropriate items.[33] Third, subsidies could provide benefits to firms that would have undertaken the activities even in the absence of the subsidy, raising the budget cost without providing any additional security measures. And fourth, subsidies financed from general revenue are in effect paid for by the entire population. As discussed earlier, the fairness and feasibility of that approach is debatable, especially in face of the dramatic deterioration in the outlook of the federal budget since the September attacks and the recognition that other pressing needs in the war on terrorism will put increased pressure on the budget even without subsidizing private sector protective measures.[34]

Toward a Mixed System: Minimum Regulatory Standards and Insurance

Though all government interventions have their shortcomings, which vary in importance from sector to sector, one longer-term approach appears to be the least undesirable and most cost-effective: a combination of regulatory standards and antiterrorism insurance. Such a mixed system should only be applied when government intervention is warranted; as emphasized earlier, a key question in evaluating that threshold is the degree to which the government action will reduce overall exposure to the risk of major terrorism (rather than merely shift it from one target to another with a comparable level of damage).

A mixed regulatory/insurance system is employed in many other circumstances, such as owning a home or driving a car. Local building codes specify minimum standards that homes must meet. But mortgages generally require that homes also carry home insurance, and insurance companies provide incentives for improvements beyond the building code level, for example, by offering a reduction in the premiums they charge if the homeowner installs a security system. Similarly, governments specify minimum standards that drivers must meet in order to operate a motor vehicle. But they also require drivers to carry liability insurance for accidents arising out of the operation of their vehicles. Meanwhile, insurance companies provide incentives for safer driving by charging higher premiums to those with poorer driving records.

To be sure, crucial differences exist between the terrorist case and these other examples. For one thing, stable actuarial data exist for home and auto accidents, but not for terrorist attacks. Nonetheless, it may be possible for insurers to distinguish risks of loss based on differences in damage exposures, given a terrorist incident. Some financial firms are already trying to devise basic frameworks for evaluating such risks.[35]

In short, a mixed system of minimum standards coupled with an insurance mandate can encourage actors not only to act safely, but also to seek innovative ways to reduce the costs of achieving any given level of safety.[36] (In some cases, a formal insurance requirement may not be necessary because lenders already require terrorism insurance to be carried before extending a loan, and a government mandate is thus superfluous.) The presence of minimum regulatory standards also helps to attenuate the moral hazard effect from insurance and can offer courts some guidance in determining negligence under the liability laws (see appendix A for further discussion of legal liability issues).[37]

A mixed system also has the advantage of being flexible, a key virtue in an arena where new threats seem to be "discovered" repeatedly. In situations in which insurance firms are particularly unlikely to provide proper incentives to the private sector for efficient risk reduction (for example, because insurers lack experience in these areas), regulation can play a larger role. But when insurance firms are able to devise incentives for innovative and cost-effective security measures, regulation could play a smaller role.

The mixed system of regulatory standards and antiterrorism insurance seems well suited for three kinds of risks, beginning with security at chemical and biological plants. Such plants contain materials that could be used as part of a catastrophic terrorist attack and should therefore be subjected to more stringent security requirements than other commercial facilities. But the regulatory standards could be supplemented by insurance coverage, which would then allow insurance firms to provide incentives for more innovative security measures.

Second, the mixed approach is appropriate for buildings that house thousands of people. The federal government could supplement existing building codes for large commercial buildings with minimum performance-based antiterrorism standards. These in turn could be supplemented by requiring the owners of buildings to obtain antiterrorism insurance covering some multiple of the value of their property. Even if the regulators decided that basic antiterrorism insurance premiums should not vary by type of building (for the reasons mentioned), they could still allow the basic premium to be adjusted for building improvements that reduce the probability or severity of an attack (such as protecting the air intake system or reinforcing the building structure).

Third, some regulatory measures may be warranted for critical telecommunications and cyber infrastructure, at least temporarily. For example, performance-oriented regulatory steps could perhaps require critical systems to be able to withstand mock cyberattacks (with the nature of the cyberattack varying from firm to firm). Given the ease with which mock attacks and tests could be conducted (which could provide a basis for pricing the insurance), an insurance requirement may also be feasible and beneficial; insurance firms today already employ experts to advise insured firms on how to reduce their exposure to cyberattacks. To be consistent with our thresholds for government action, government intervention should occur only in cases of infrastructure components that are critical to human safety or whose disruption would cause systemic economic harm.

Our case for a mixed system of minimum standards and insurance, it should be emphasized, is a "rebuttable" one. In other words, it is a first choice over the longer term, but it can and should be supplemented or replaced when there is evidence that other approaches would be more efficient or when there are significant externalities associated with a given type of terrorism.

Furthermore, as noted earlier in the chapter, the capacity of the insurance industry to play the role envisioned for it in this mixed system is somewhat unclear and may depend in part on whether the federal government provides some kind of reinsurance in the short run. It will also take time for the industry to develop appropriate ways of pricing policies covering potentially catastrophic attacks.

Finally, the degree of government intervention should clearly vary by circumstance. For example, consider the difference between security at a mall and security at a chemical facility. Poor security at a mall does not pose the same scale of harm as poor security at a chemical facility. The products of chemical plants could be used as *inputs* in a terrorist attack, and therefore the facilities warrant more aggressive government intervention than shopping malls. Thus security regulations for chemical plants may make sense, even if they do not for shopping malls.

A critical challenge is deciding how extensive government regulation should be. It is one thing to set standards for commercial facilities such as chemical and biological plants. But should the government attempt to provide antiterrorism regulations for *all* commercial buildings? For hospitals? For universities? Where does the regulatory process stop? As we have argued throughout this analysis, the focus should be on reducing the risk of terrorist attacks with large-scale human or economic impact. Hence policymakers should proceed carefully in extending regulations beyond the areas delineated in the preceding chapters.

Coordinating Government Intervention

Who should set the standards? Because terrorism almost by definition involves potentially significant externalities for the nation as a whole, we believe there is a presumptive case favoring minimum federal standards, which states and municipalities could strengthen if they so desire. But simply saying that the responsibility belongs to the federal government does not fully answer the question. As we highlight in chapter 7, numerous federal agencies have jurisdiction over different parts of the U.S. economy.

To prevent a regulatory turf war, as well as to ensure a coordinated federal response, the new Office of Homeland Security should provide a regulatory road map, with assignments to specific agencies to deal with specific threats. The office should coordinate its activities with the Office of Information and Regulatory Affairs (OIRA) of the Office of Management and Budget (OMB). OIRA is the division responsible for overseeing the regulatory activities of executive branch agencies. In late 2001, OIRA developed a "prompt letter" through which it plans to suggest to agencies new rules that should be adopted or changes in existing rules that may be warranted. We can think of no better use of the prompt letter than to suggest regulations, developed and coordinated through the Office of Homeland Security, that agencies might introduce or tighten to deal cost-effectively with the terrorist threat.

An Efficient Response to Terrorist Threats in the Public Sector

Since the government will have primary responsibility for minimizing terrorist access to the United States and mitigating the costs of any attacks that do occur, another important policy question is how to allocate the implementation and cost of homeland security measures within the *public sector*. For example, many state and local governments will need to expand their hazardous materials response teams, increase police forces, and undertake other steps in response to the threats underscored by the September 11 attacks. How should such costs be financed?

Traditional models of fiscal federalism suggest that the federal government should finance those activities that have significant spatial externalities (that is, in which the costs or benefits of the activity spill over to other geographic areas), and that state and local governments should finance those activities with limited or no spatial externalities.[38] Thus national defense lies in the federal domain, whereas local police activities are the responsibility of lower levels of government.

Many antiterrorism measures within the public sector, however, appear difficult to classify. Are they national defense (and therefore a federal expense) or traditional policing (and therefore a state and local concern)? For example, expanding the number of local police may help to identify and prevent terrorist activities, but it can also reduce local crime. So who should pay for the expansion? As with private sector activities, several criteria may help to determine the nature of the intervention within the public sector:

—To what degree will state and local governments undertake insufficient antiterrorism efforts in the absence of a federal mandate or subsidy?

—To what degree does the measure provide collateral benefits to the local geographical area?

—To what degree will incompatible state and local regulations or approaches impose additional costs on individuals and firms (including any costs related to displacing terrorist activity from one area to another), and to what extent will they allow valuable experimentation with various antiterrorism measures?

—How fair is the expected outcome? Will society accept the consequences of the action on the distribution of income or wealth?

Although the appropriate response will vary from issue to issue, the general principle we adopt for public sector activities is that the federal government should be responsible for measures that are clearly, primarily, and specifically linked to reducing the threat or severity of terrorist attacks. Measures that primarily provide collateral benefits to the local area should generally be financed by local or state governments, even if they provide some antiterrorism benefits.

One of the crucial factors to evaluate is the degree to which a spatial externality is involved: the larger the spatial externality, the more likely it is that federal financing is justified. Thus public health activities should be financed at least in part by the federal government, given the communicability of disease and therefore the significant spatial externality involved. Similarly, basic research—for example, on vaccines and innovative antiterrorism devices—would have significant benefits for people across the entire nation and therefore should be financed by the federal government. Security measures at the nation's ports should be financed at least in part by the federal government, since the ports are a gateway to the nation as a whole and inadequate security could allow terrorist materials to gain entry and be dispersed to remote geographical areas. But expanded police patrols should be financed by state and local governments, since the patrols largely if not entirely guard against attacks that would be confined to the immediate area.

In summary, the federal government should undertake those antiterrorism measures that have clear national benefits, but it should not finance state and local government activities with substantial local benefits (such as hiring additional police or firefighters). The larger the collateral local benefit in relation to the antiterrorism benefit, the smaller the federal share should be. Such an approach avoids excessive federal subsidization of activities that have significant local benefits.

Conclusions

Policymakers concerned with homeland security must carefully balance the gains from deterring the number and severity of future terrorist attacks against the costs of the security measures. To prevent attacks that would involve the loss of thousands of lives, or widespread economic harm, government action is warranted. Over the longer term, a promising approach for such action is a mixed regulatory and insurance system. This approach ensures that costs are borne by the users and producers of a service, rather than by the population as a whole, and thus avoids "gold plating" the antiterrorism activities. It also seeks to provide some benefit—for example, in terms of reduced insurance premiums—from undertaking additional security measures.

Public sector homeland security activities should be financed by the federal government when they involve a specific antiterrorism measure or address significant spatial externalities, but state and local governments should finance antiterrorism activities that provide substantial collateral local benefits (in addition to reducing the probability or severity of a terrorist attack). These guidelines will need to evolve over time as more experience accumulates.

They underscore two of the three general themes of this book regarding how to achieve homeland security at reasonable economic cost: security measures should provide some benefit (for example, reduced waiting times or insurance premiums) to induce additional security precautions, and stakeholders should pay for most such measures. As earlier chapters make plain, the third theme is that information technologies will play an important role in promoting security at reasonable cost.

7

ORGANIZING FOR SUCCESS

Ultimate success in protecting the American homeland against terrorist attack will depend to a significant extent on how the U.S. government is organized to meet this threat. [1] As Dwight D. Eisenhower famously remarked at the end of his long and distinguished career, although "organization cannot make a genius out of an incompetent, ... disorganization can scarcely fail to result in inefficiency and can easily lead to disaster."[2] The organizational challenge of homeland security is profound, for there are few government activities that are at once so crucial and so difficult to manage. Responsibility is widely dispersed, not only within the federal government but also among federal, state, and local authorities, and the private sector. Moreover, unlike, say, the agencies responsible for national security policy, these units lack a culture of cooperation such as the National Security Council (NSC) has nurtured for half a century.

The number of federal departments, agencies, and offices involved in homeland security is difficult to quantify. According to the Office of Management and Budget, nearly 70 agencies spend money on counterterrorist activities, and that excludes the Defense and State Departments as well as the intelligence community![3]

One organizational chart of federal government agencies that bear some responsibility for homeland security depicts 130 separate boxes.[4] Even by more discriminating accounting standards, anywhere between 40 and 50 agencies are believed to be involved in the homeland security effort—ranging from the departments of state, defense, treasury, justice, transportation, health and human services, and agriculture, to intelligence agencies like the Central Intelligence Agency and National Security Agency, to law enforcement agencies like the Federal Bureau of Investigation, the Secret Service, the Drug Enforcement Agency, and the Bureau of Alcohol, Tobacco, and Firearms, to agencies monitoring points of entry into the United States like the Border Control, the Coast Guard, the Customs Service, and the Immigration and Naturalization Service, to agencies responsible for responding to an attack, like the Federal Emergency Management Agency (FEMA), the Centers for Disease Control and Prevention, the National Guard Bureau, and the Pentagon's Joint Task Force for Homeland Defense.

This diffusion of responsibility is inherent in the problem these entities seek to tackle. Homeland security is, by its very nature, a highly decentralized activity, one where success depends on a multitude of individuals at the outer edges of activity making good decisions. A customs service agent sensed something amiss with a car traveling from Canada to the United States in December 1999 and discovered its trunk loaded with explosive materials designed to blow up Los Angeles Airport at the turn of the millennium. A flight instructor found it suspicious that a student was interested only in steering a commercial jetliner, not in taking off or landing, and then reported his suspicion to law enforcement authorities. A firefighter yelled at people coming up from the World Trade Center subway station to go back down, before himself climbing up the stairs to the fires burning on the seventy-fifth floor of one of the towers. A doctor reexamined the X ray of a postal worker and diagnosed inhalation anthrax in time for an effective antibiotic treatment to be administered. A flight attendant noticed a passenger lighting a match near his feet and acted swiftly to prevent him from detonating a bomb in his shoe. Ultimately, the security of the American homeland depends upon good decisions like these by the many hundreds of thousands of so-called first responders—the border guards, immigration officers, and customs agents; the doctors, nurses, firefighters, and police officers—who guard our front lines. Managing, coordinating, leading, and mobilizing these people so that their individual decisions add up to a nation more secure, better prepared, and more responsive to the terrorist threat—that is the organizational challenge of homeland security.

Organizational Approaches

There are two basic approaches to organizing the federal government for homeland security. First, a single agency—either an existing department or a new one—can be designated to take the lead in preventing, protecting against, and responding to a terrorist attack. A second approach focuses on interagency (and intergovernmental) coordination, in which a single entity, most likely located in the White House, coordinates the myriad of agencies responsible for different aspects of homeland security and brings them together to work as a team.

The Lead Agency Approach

The Clinton administration organized its counterterrorism efforts largely around the lead agency concept. Its first organizational effort, set forth in Presidential Decision Directive (PDD) 39 of June 1995, assigned lead agency responsibility to the Department of Justice for addressing terrorism at home. This assignment was retained three years later, when as part of PDD-62, the administration created the position of national coordinator for security, infrastructure protection, and counterterrorism based in the NSC. This person's task was to help run the interagency process, but without having any direct authority over individual agencies or any operational role. Responsibility for counterterrorism, including all facets of homeland security, continued to rest with the agencies.

The diffusion of responsibility inherent in this approach may have been adequate to respond to limited terrorist incidents, but it is wholly inadequate for meeting the much more difficult challenge of catastrophic terrorism. Hence, even before September 11, a variety of national commissions examined U.S. government organization for counterterrorism and found it wanting. The most comprehensive set of organizational proposals was put forward by the Commission on National Security/21st Century, better known as the Hart-Rudman Commission, after its two cochairmen, former senators Gary Hart and Warren Rudman. In its third and final report

Figure 7-1. *Department of Homeland Security*

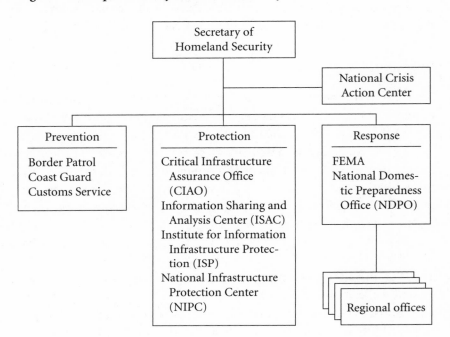

released in March 2001, the commission proposed the creation of a new National Homeland Security Agency (NHSA) by merging a number of U.S. government agencies responsible for different homeland security tasks into a consolidated whole.[5] These ideas have since been taken up by Congress, notably by Representative Mac Thornberry (R-Texas) in the House and Senators Joe Lieberman (D-Conn.) and Arlen Specter (R-Pa.) in the Senate.[6]

The basic concept is the creation of a cabinet-level department with overall responsibility for preventing, protecting against, and responding to a terrorist attack (see figure 7-1). The prevention function would be accomplished by transferring the Coast Guard, Customs Service, and Border Patrol to the new department. The protection function would be fulfilled by adding offices responsible for protecting critical infrastructure now housed in the Federal Bureau of Investigation (FBI) and the Commerce Department. The Federal Emergency Management Agency (FEMA), including its

10 regional offices, and the FBI's National Domestic Preparedness Office would form the core of the response functions. Overall the new department and its head would be assigned the lead homeland security role in the federal government. It would be responsible for planning, coordinating, integrating, and overseeing the implementation of the various homeland security activities pursued by other U.S. government agencies, as well as state and local authorities.

The strengths of this approach are many. Assigning clear responsibility for homeland security to a single agency provides clarity in an otherwise diffuse landscape of interests and capabilities. Accountability should thereby be enhanced. Merging critical functions dealing with frontier security, infrastructure protection, and emergency response into distinct directorates should ease communications and enhance effective implementation of agreed policy both within and probably among the directorates. And empowering the new entity by providing it with direct budgetary authority and political responsibility should make the agency a major player in the overall homeland security effort.

But against these benefits stand notable weaknesses. The homeland security mission is one that by definition involves many more entities than can be brought under a single roof. Left outside will necessarily be key agencies, including: the Department of Defense and its innumerable assets for defending against and responding to an attack; the Department of Justice and the FBI, which are responsible for domestic surveillance and law enforcement; the Department of Health and Human Services and the Centers for Disease Control and Prevention, responsible for detecting and responding to a bioterrorist attack; the Central Intelligence Agency and other parts of the intelligence community, responsible for tracking terrorists and the materials they might bring into the country to do us harm; not to mention state and local government authorities. Consolidation may better focus some homeland security efforts, but it cannot include all or even most.

With many important functions left out of the consolidated agency, there will still be a need for effective coordination. But assigning that function to the head of a new homeland security entity, as some propose, does not appear promising, even if that official were given cabinet rank. A secretary of homeland security, with direct authority for some (but not most) relevant governmental activity, would likely be perceived as being partial toward the functions she or he supervised. This would create resistance by peers with major authorities of their own (the attorney general, for example, or the secretary of health and human services) just as the secretary of state—repeatedly called upon to exercise government-wide foreign affairs leadership—comes up against the Department of Defense and the intelligence community. The secretary of the treasury has fared somewhat better in the economic realm but has typically not been able to lead on budget policy, or on international trade. Nor is the coordination problem solved by making the new secretary a member of the NSC and turning the coordination role over to the council, as Hart-Rudman proposes, since many of the domestic agencies involved in the homeland security effort would still be excluded.

Coordination is difficult to achieve through any arrangement, but it tends to work better when the leader is perceived as an honest broker or can invoke the authority of the White House. If the coordinator is seen as a competitor, other agencies whose cooperation is crucial are likely to balk at following its lead, and bureaucratic fights over turf become pervasive. But the diffusion of power over homeland security throughout the U.S. government requires that someone pull the different strands together into an integrated approach.

The Interagency Coordination Approach

An alternative is to establish a focal point in the Executive Office of the President. Experience suggests two ways of doing so. One is the appointment of a homeland security czar, a person who, much like the drug czar who heads the Office of National Drug Control Policy (ONDCP), would pull together the numerous aspects of homeland defense into a coherent whole. Another is the creation of a White House-based council, which is the approach adopted by the Bush administration.

The czar approach has been championed by the Gilmore Commission, which recommended the establishment of a coordination entity within the Executive Office of the President.[7] Drawing on the ONDCP model, it would have the following characteristics:[8]

—A strong cabinet-level agency would be established within the Executive Office of the President.

—The agency would be led by a director and selected senior staff that are subject to Senate confirmation. The director would also be a member of the National Security Council for counterterrorism-related matters.

—The senior staff would be required by law to be wholly apolitical.

—The agency would be responsible for producing the nation's homeland security strategy, and an accompanying budget to ensure its implementation.

—The director would have the authority to decertify any agency's budget that fails to meet the requirements of the strategy.

—The agency would also be responsible for producing a system of performance measurements to track progress in reducing the threat to homeland security.

—The agency would be independently accountable to the Congress and the public and regularly report on how it is carrying out its responsibilities.

—The agency would be provided with the resources necessary to get the job done through its own budget and dedicated staff (including, in particular, its own strategic planning, budget, public affairs, and congressional affairs staffs).

—The director would be empowered to call interagency meetings to address critical issues and threats.

—And, most important, all these powers and responsibilities would be specifically set forth in a statute.

Past experience with the czar model suggests that this approach is unlikely to be fully effective. Even the strongest drug czars (including William Bennett under the first President George Bush and General Barry McCaffrey under President Bill Clinton) were never able to wrest control over policy and funding from the individual agencies responsible for implementing drug policy. The ability to develop a national drug control strategy helped the drug czar shape overall policy, while his power to decertify agency budgets provided some leverage over programs. But these powers alone did not bring him overall control. The national strategy became a largely aspirational document with only very loose ties to budgetary priorities. The decertification power proved more effective in theory than in practice (McCaffrey was the only ONDCP head to use it, and then only once). Even though ONDCP is nominally in charge, interagency coordination efforts have not always been effective. And as a federal agency, ONDCP has no control over state and local government efforts that are crucial to combating drugs.

An alternative to the czar model is to base coordination on the experience of previous policy-coordinating councils located in the White House, particularly the National Security and National Economic Councils. This is, of course, the approach adopted by President Bush in the aftermath of the September 11 attacks, when he brought former Pennsylvania Governor Tom Ridge to Washington to head a new structure and process.

As spelled out in the president's Executive Order, the main coordinating body is the new Homeland Security Council (HSC), which is composed of the president, vice president, secretary of the treasury, secretary of defense, attorney general, secretary of health and human services, secretary of transportation, FEMA director, FBI director, director of central intelligence, and director of the Homeland Security Office. As is the case for the NSC and the National Economic Council (NEC) in their respective spheres, the HSC is "responsible for advising and assisting the President with respect to all aspects of homeland security. The Council shall serve as the mechanism for ensuring coordination of homeland security-related activities of executive departments and agencies and effective development and implementation of homeland security policies."[9] Since its establishment, the HSC has met as often as twice a week, with the president in attendance.

The HSC process is staffed by Ridge's Office of Homeland Security (OHS), which plays a role akin to that of the NSC staff. Indeed, the initial Homeland Security Presidential Directive (HSPD-1) sets forth an organizational structure for the OHS and details an HSC process that is modeled on the NSC process, as detailed in National Security Presidential Decision No. 1 (NSPD-1), signed in February 2001.[10] Thus, like the NSC, the HSC is supported by an interagency structure that includes the HSC Principals Committee (chaired by Ridge and composed of all HSC members other than the president and vice president, who are represented by their respective chiefs of staff), the HSC Deputies Committee (chaired by Ridge's deputy, Admiral Steven Abbott, and composed of the deputies to the HSC members), and 22 HSC policy-coordinating committees (PCCs) dealing with such issues as detection, surveillance, and intelligence; law enforce-

Figure 7-2. *Office of Homeland Security*

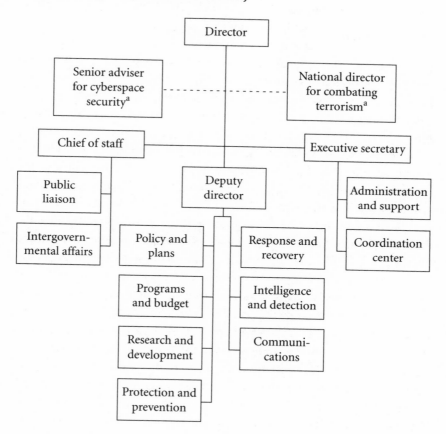

a. These positions also report to the assistant to the president for National Security Affairs.

ment; weapons of mass destruction; consequence management; and economic consequences. Each PCC is chaired by an OHS senior director.

The Homeland Security Office also mimics the organizational structure of the NSC staff (see figure 7-2) to a large extent. There is one deputy director and two other senior officials (the president's special adviser for cybersecurity and the national director for combating terrorism) who report jointly to Ridge and to the national security adviser. Issues are addressed by ten directorates, including seven for specific policy areas. Each directorate is headed by a senior director, who is also a special assistant to the president. The seven policy directorates—dealing with such issues as protection and prevention, response and recovery, intelligence and detection, and programs and budgets—report to Ridge through the deputy director. The OHS also has a chief of staff (who supervises the directorates dealing with public liaison and intergovernmental affairs) and an executive secretary responsible for administrative matters. Finally, Ridge has set up a national coordinating center to analyze and share intelligence and other data about terrorist threats and vulnerabilities and to coordinate agency responses in case of an attack.[11]

These organizational structures and interagency processes put Ridge in a strong position. As the person designated by the president to manage the overall coordinating process, Ridge enjoys tremendous power within the executive branch that, if employed wisely, can help overcome many of the organizational difficulties inherent in the homeland security task, including especially the wide dispersal of authority and capabilities that need to be brought together. By chairing all interagency committees, Ridge and his office have the power to set the agenda, convene meetings, and forge a consensus. But wielding that power effectively will require subtlety on Ridge's part. He needs to gain the cooperation of the many cabinet secretaries and agency directors who ultimately will have responsibility for taking the actions that make our homeland safe. Neither Ridge nor anyone on his staff will have the authority to tell others what to do—action must come from the acquiescence, if not support, of Ridge's peers themselves and the strong backing of the president.

But even the best coordination processes may not be enough to ensure a smooth-functioning and effective organization. There are inherent inefficiencies in the dispersal of authority among many agencies, including inevitable duplication of effort and an absence of clear lines of communication and control. Accountability is more difficult to assign. Moreover, without formal authority over budgets, people, and programs, the OHS director has little more than his own leadership talent—as well as whatever empowerment he gets from the president—to get the job done. As a result, there is considerable skepticism, notably on Capitol Hill, that Ridge has the tools and power necessary for the job. "Without budgetary or statutory authority, Ridge is doomed not to succeed," former senator Hart has argued. "He will have to keep going to the Oval Office to make anything happen. Anyone who knows Washington, knows this won't work."[12]

Organizational Functions

In order to execute its mandate of helping the U.S. government detect, prepare for, prevent, respond to, and recover from terrorist attacks, the Office of Homeland Security must perform four functions effectively. First, Ridge and his staff must coordinate the U.S. government entities to ensure their individual actions combine into an effective response. Second, OHS will be primarily responsible for providing strategic direction. Third, the office must ensure that adequate resources are available to implement the strategy. Fourth, Ridge needs to be in charge of managing any crises to ensure the U.S. government responds as rapidly and effectively as possible.

Coordination

The most immediate challenge Ridge confronts is to ensure effective coordination of the many agencies and interests that have a role to play in homeland security. He needs to establish his bona fides early on and gain control of the interagency process in order to demonstrate his authority. To do so, Ridge would do well to turn to the experience of previous NSC and NEC advisers, all of whom faced similar coordination challenges.

A particularly relevant example is the role played by Robert Rubin as the first NEC adviser at the beginning of the Clinton administration. Like Ridge, Rubin was both assigned responsibility for a new coordinating council and tasked to get government moving in a policy area of top presidential priority, peopled with senior officials holding strong mandates and strong views. Had Rubin seen his role as one of issuing orders for other Clinton economic officials to carry out, his governmental life might have proved nasty, brutish, and short. Instead, he took the initiative in organizing internal debate on key issues, with a process designed to force presidential decisions, but one that assiduously reached out to the secretary and deputy secretary of the treasury, the director of the Office of Management and Budget, and the chair of the Council of Economic Advisers. He gave them something they wanted and needed—visible participation in and influence over the most important decisions of Clinton's early presidency. In so doing, he strengthened their credibility and influence within their agencies, while neatly ensconcing Rubin's NEC at the center of the economic policy process.[13]

Ridge can learn even more from the four decades-plus experience of the modern NSC. Emulating proven NSC practices, Ridge should use the HSC as an umbrella to establish a network not only of formal interagency coordinating structures such as that set up under HSPD-1, but also the crucial informal networks. History shows that the NSC processes operate most effectively when the national security adviser works closely and frequently informally with his or her key counterparts at State, Defense and, sometimes, the CIA. When Colin Powell was national security adviser in the last year of the Reagan administration, he met with Secretary of State George Shultz and Defense Secretary Frank Carlucci each day at 7:00 A.M. in his office to coordinate their day's work. Today, Condoleezza Rice has a daily telephone call at 7:15 A.M. with Vice President Dick Cheney, Secretary of State Colin Powell, and Defense Secretary Don Rumsfeld. And nearly all NSC advisers from Zbigniew Brzezinski onward have convened weekly lunches or breakfasts with their senior counterparts to work on issues in a less formal setting. Ridge should conduct similar sets of regular, informal meetings with his key counterparts, including especially the attorney general and perhaps also the defense and treasury secretaries.

Strategic Planning

In addition to pursuing effective coordination, the OHS needs to take responsibility for planning the strategic direction of the homeland security effort. In the executive order setting up the OHS, Bush directed Ridge to prepare such a strategy in cooperation with "executive departments and agencies, State and local governments, and private entities."[14] Although the national strategy will not be completed until the summer of 2002, the White House has set clear parameters for what it will contain. It is to be a long-term, truly national plan that sets strategy not just for the federal government but also for state and local government, the private sector, and U.S. citizens. It will be comprehensive. It will include the full range of activities with a clear set of priorities. It will set clear objectives and provide benchmarks and other performance measures to evaluate the strategy's implementation and determine how resources can best be allocated. Finally, the "strategy will take full account of the existing government institutions and systems for providing homeland security, such as law enforcement, public safety, public health, and emergency management."[15]

Developing a comprehensive homeland security strategy has definite advantages. It provides the federal government, state and local authorities, and private entities and citizens with a clear statement of objectives and policy on how best to secure the American homeland against terrorist attack, how to organize and implement this effort, and how to budget for it. Finally, a strategy that delineates benchmarks for achieving specific goals should enable the OHS to determine with some degree of precision how well agencies are implementing the strategy over time.

At the same time, a national strategy of this kind is likely to be useful only up to a point. Unlike the case of drugs and many other policy areas, homeland security is a vast enterprise not readily reducible to a single strategic framework. While broad statements of principle, major strategic imperatives, and large organizational requirements can of course be detailed in a national strategy, no single document is likely to be sufficiently comprehensive to guide the entire effort all on its own. It can set direction, delimit parameters, and provide overall coherence, but a single strategy cannot prescribe every important goal, strategy, and action that needs to be taken. The greatest concern, however, is that the effort to produce a single, coherent statement is bound to generate pressures for a document that accommodates the views of major agencies and interests rather than one that sharply delineates the choices our nation confronts. More often than not, documents like these make for bland reading because too many hands are involved in their drafting, and too many concerns need to be reconciled.

This suggests the possible utility of a supplementary approach, one modeled on past and current practice in the national security arena. Rather than issuing a fully fleshed-out strategy for the entire government, Ridge should commission analyses of a series of first-order issues that will require presidential decisions. This would involve the issuance of homeland security study directives (HSSDs) tasking interagency groups to present specific options, defined not as agency preferences but as real, alternative ways of addressing key problems. Some HSSDs could address questions of structure and process: organization; budget authority; and intelligence collection, sharing, and analysis. Others could address particular broad tasks: prevention, damage limitation, countering particular threats such as biological and chemical agents, and cooperative law enforcement. The options developed in such studies would be debated at HSC meetings chaired by the president, followed by his choosing among them. His decision would subsequently be codified in an HSPD signed by him.

Commissioning such policy reviews while the Homeland Security Office and council are relatively new would serve several related goals. It would give the adviser the initiative in policy development. It would engage other departments and agencies in the critical task of formulating realistic choices. It would increase the chances for well-integrated policy. And it would connect the adviser/HSC to the president at a time when the chief executive is giving top priority and attention to homeland security issues. It would also be a potent device to meet the need for what Ashton Carter labels "*program* coordination . . . a multiyear, multiagency effort to develop tactics, technology, and where required new institutions for the ongoing struggle against catastrophic terrorism."[16]

Once a series of HSPDs has been issued and key questions have been decided, there would be a stronger basis for formulating an integrated homeland security strategy. The HSSM/HSPD process works best if it is used as a way to decide the main provisions of the national strategy. This sequential approach to strategic planning would avoid the blandness likely to result from producing a consensus document from scratch, since the critical issues will have been thrashed out through an analytically more challenging process. At the same time, the government is more likely to be guided by an integrated strategy designed to pull key presidential decisions into a coherent and comprehensive whole.

Budgeting

The wide dispersal of homeland security competence within the federal bureaucracy means that budget authority is widely dispersed as well. Dozens of agencies and several thousand individual programs have pieces of the homeland security budget. For fiscal 2003, the Bush administration identified over 20 departments and agencies that have requested a total of $37.7 billion for homeland security–related functions. How should this overall budget process be structured? Given the way Washington works, the role of individual agencies and their congressional appropriators will inevitably be great. The administration may present a single budget, but appropriations will go to the many that are ultimately responsible for spending the funds. The key role for a central authority like OHS thus comes in drawing up the budget that is submitted to the Hill, and (to the extent possible) influencing bargaining with Congress over proposed changes.

Unfortunately, Tom Ridge has been given only a weak formal role in the budgetary process. According to the president's Executive Order, Ridge "shall review and provide advice to the heads of departments and agencies for such programs [and] provide advice to the [OMB] Director on the level and use of funding in departments and agencies for homeland security–related activities and, prior to the Director's forwarding of the proposed annual budget submission to the President for transmittal to the Congress, shall certify to the Director the funding levels that [he] believes are necessary and appropriate for the homeland security–related activities of the executive branch."[17] Thus, for the fiscal 2003 budget, Ridge was provided the opportunity to review the agency budget submissions. OMB people worked directly with Ridge's office to identify spending priorities and find ways to increase spending in a number of key areas.[18] Ridge told the New York Times, "Everything I asked for, I got," suggesting that at least under current conditions the advisory process can produce results.[19]

It may well be that when the threat is both immediate and clear, Ridge's advisory role will suffice. Getting agencies to spend resources for homeland security is not a problem. The obverse is more likely, with agencies seeking to sell some of their programs as a contribution to homeland security, knowing that in a tight budget climate that is where the money is. But organizations must function in many climates, including one where the incentive to spend on programs protecting the homeland is less, as was the case prior to September 11. In such a situation, an advisory role such as the one Ridge currently enjoys is unlikely to be enough.

To ensure OHS's continued influence over the budget, Ridge needs to have real authority over the budget process within the executive branch. Since he cannot take away actual budgetary control from the agencies that are responsible for executing the programs the Congress funds, he needs to do the second-best thing and ally himself closely to OMB, which bears responsibility for drawing up the president's annual budget submission to

Congress. Mitchell Daniels, the OMB director, recognized the importance of doing so: "The president made it clear from the beginning that when it came to Tom Ridge, we were supposed to be his budget office."[20] To institutionalize this arrangement, it would be useful to appoint one person to serve both as Ridge's budget chief and as a new associate director of OMB for homeland security. This dual-hatting will give OHS a unique status in the budget process. Not only will it have the overarching budgetary view that only a coordinating office like OHS can have, but by being an integral part of the OMB process it can exert major, if not actually decisive, influence over the final outcome.

Crisis Management

The final major function of OHS is to help manage crises, especially in the event of a major terrorist attack. The current system gives Ridge broad crisis management authority. According to the Executive Order, Ridge will be "primarily responsible for coordinating the domestic response efforts of all departments and agencies in the event of an imminent terrorist threat and during and in the immediate aftermath of a terrorist attack within the United States and shall be the principal point of contact."[21] Such a centralized system can be highly effective, as seen in the government's response to the crash of an American Airlines jet in Queens, New York, in November 2001. Within minutes of the crash, Ridge had called a meeting with the attorney general, FBI director, transportation secretary, and others to determine whether terrorism might be the cause and what the appropriate response should be. For two hours, the group sifted through incoming information, considered possible courses of action, and coordinated support for the on-the-ground response effort. Once terrorism had been ruled out as a likely cause of the crash, standard response procedures for airplane accidents went into effect, and Ridge withdrew from any further involvement.[22] In the future, Ridge's coordination efforts will be supported by an operations center somewhat akin to the White House Situation Room. The center, which is staffed by people detailed from a wide variety of agencies, will analyze and share data from multiple sources and will act as the communication hub in case of a crisis.[23]

Centralization at the top is necessary to coordinate an effective response to any incident that requires the involvement of more than a handful of agencies. The principal organizational question is whether such centralization should be extended down to the site of the actual incident. One useful suggestion is to create a cadre of people, drawn from various agencies but responsive to Ridge's office, who would be sent into the field to coordinate at least the federal government's response efforts. These would be Ridge's people, reporting directly to him at the center, and they would be in charge on the ground.[24]

Organizational Adjustments

President Bush was right to emphasize the importance of interagency coordination. The wide dispersal of authority and competence requires that someone very senior be put in charge of pulling these disparate strands together into a coherent whole. The appointment of Tom Ridge, a close friend and powerful political ally of the president's, signaled the importance President Bush attaches to the issue of homeland security. During the first months of operation, Ridge has gotten a functioning organization off the ground, and the coordinating effort appears to be working well. At the same time, to enhance his stature and authority, both within the executive branch and in his relations with Congress, state and local authorities, and the American public, it is important for his position to be enacted into law and for his appointment to be confirmed by the U.S. Senate.

In addition to enhancement of Ridge's authority, structural adjustments are required in some agencies to reflect the new demands of homeland security. This is particularly the case for agencies responsible for securing our borders. Multiple law enforcement and intelligence agencies need to be better coordinated as well. Moreover, given its vast resources and capabilities, the Defense Department will also need to take on a greater role for securing the homeland against terrorist attack. Finally, Congress needs to examine ways in which it might be reorganized to meet the demands of homeland security.

Statutory Authority

As a presidential adviser primarily responsible for ensuring effective coordination, Ridge must realize that his power in Washington will be ephemeral if it is not constantly nurtured and effectively protected. Battles will inevitably loom with Cabinet colleagues. He needs to be careful about which ones he chooses to fight—and he must make sure that he wins most of them, particularly during his first year.

Unfortunately, the early returns are not uniformly encouraging. While he worked hard with others to create a national terrorist alert system, the ultimate authority for determining alert levels was vested in the attorney general, even though the OHS director was arguably better placed to do so. And whereas Ridge championed the establishment of a new, independent border agency through the consolidation of the Coast Guard, Customs Service, Border Patrol, and Agricultural Quarantine Inspection Agency, he was ultimately forced to join a consensus in favor of something far less, as we discuss below. If such defeats—real and perceived—become a pattern, Ridge will lose credibility. Over time, few will defer to Ridge, and fewer still are likely to follow his lead.

While statutory authority for White House advisory positions is something presidents naturally tend to shun, such authority is appropriate in Ridge's case. Unlike his counterparts at the NSC and NEC, he has operational responsibilities, and is not simply a policy coordinator. The closest parallel is that of drug czar or the OMB director. Ridge has developed a budget. He is the prime public spokesman in his area of activity. He needs to be made formally accountable to Congress, both out of respect for legislative authority and to increase overall governmental capacity to respond to the challenge of catastrophic terrorism. Moreover, under current circumstances statutory authority may be the best—if not the only—way for Ridge to gain the stature he needs to get the job done. He should have cabinet rank. At the same time, legislation establishing the position of Homeland Security Council and the OHS should give maximum operating flexibility to the president to design its organization and mission.

A Federal Border Agency

Responsibility for securing and monitoring the people and cargo that enter the United States is dispersed among several agencies. As far as people are concerned, consular officers employed by the State Department at U.S. embassies abroad determine the eligibility of foreigners to receive visas and issue them to those who meet the legal criteria. The Immigration and Naturalization Service (INS) checks people at the border, and the Border

Patrol surveys the frontier to ensure no one enters beyond authorized cross-ing points. Goods and conveyors are checked by the Coast Guard at sea and by customs and agricultural inspectors at border crossings and all other ports of entry. Intercepting unidentified aircraft and (in the future) missiles is the responsibility of the Defense Department. Thus no fewer than six departments (State, Justice, Treasury, Transportation, Agriculture, and Defense) help secure the U.S. border against intrusion of people and mate-rials that could do us harm.

This dispersed responsibility led Governor Ridge to propose merging at least some of the agencies into a federal border agency: "When you come into the United States, multiple faces of the federal government meet you. And I think we ought to have one face at the border."[25] Accordingly, in December 2001 Ridge proposed the creation of the National Border Administration, which would consist of the Coast Guard, the Customs Service, the enforcement arm of the Immigration and Naturalization Service (including the Border Patrol), and the Agriculture Quarantine Inspection program.[26] According to a White House white paper proposing this consolidation, the new agency's core mission "would be to manage the physical entry and exit of all people, goods, and vehicles into the United States by air, land, or sea, and in so doing to prevent, preempt, and deter ter-rorist infiltration or the introduction of weapons of mass destruction."[27] By bringing these agencies under one roof, a more streamlined and integrated border monitoring effort would likely result. For that reason, it would prob-ably be advisable to include in the consolidation the new Transportation Security Agency (which is responsible for monitoring what goes onto com-mercial aircraft) and perhaps the consular functions in the State Department.

Ridge's proposal met with predictable resistance. None of the depart-ments wanted to give up control over border security functions currently under their management. And all of the agencies were concerned that their duties not related to terrorism would receive shorter shrift if they were merged into a border agency whose primary task would be to prevent ter-rorists and weapons from entering the United States. Turf wars are inevitable when structural change is proposed. As one White House official told the Washington Post, "If we go ahead with a new border agency, it will mean ripping big organizations out of two or three Cabinet departments, and no Cabinet secretary I have ever seen wants to give up part of his department."[28] And the candidates for consolidation, fearful that a merger will eventually lead to their extinction, are not above arguing that they should be maintained as distinct entities because they have been around for a long time. Customs Service officials responded to Ridge's proposal by emphasizing that their agency dates back to 1789 and was established by the fifth act of the first Congress!

There may indeed be some historical logic to the disparate organizational placement of these border agencies. But the current case for the status quo is extraordinarily weak. Not a single one of them is central to the mission of its cabinet-agency home—not the Customs Service, not the INS enforcement arm, not U.S. Department of Agriculture quarantine inspection, not the Coast Guard. The cabinet secretaries now allegedly threatened gave no serious attention to any of them prior to September 11. It may be turf they are guarding, but for them it is not prime turf. And as Ridge said in taking up his post, "The only turf we should be worried about protecting is the turf we stand on."[29]

Ridge was right. But the combined departmental opposition to the creation of a federal border agency may have proven too much to overcome. In March, a different proposal emerged from the HSC that would bring the Customs Service into the Justice Department and merge it with the enforcement arm of INS into a separate agency. Even though this idea fell far short of what Ridge had originally demanded, it gained the HSC's unanimous backing.[30] Despite such unanimity, this proposal is little more than a half measure. Not only does the new agency exclude the Coast Guard, but by placing it within the Justice Department the problematic parochialism characterizing border security efforts in the past will be preserved. Therefore the president should support Governor Ridge's original proposal and send up legislation to Capitol Hill that would create a federal border agency to meet the demands and threats of the twenty-first century.

Law Enforcement/Intelligence Cooperation

The need to coordinate intelligence and law enforcement efforts was critically underscored by the September 11 attacks. Although it is far from clear that better coordination could have prevented an attack about which very little was known, there can be no doubt of the importance of such coordination. Part of the answer, as we argued above, lies in improving the ways information is shared and diverse databases are accessed. It would clearly help if a state trooper tapping into a database checking on a driver of a speeding car were informed that the person was being sought by federal law enforcement authorities. Part of the answer also lies in better coordination of the large number of law enforcement and intelligence agencies at the center. Finally, it may also require some reorganization among agencies—especially at the federal law enforcement level.

Coordination among law enforcement and intelligence agencies is not a new issue. Throughout the past two decades, and especially during the 1990s, issues like drug trafficking, international crime, and terrorism have been increasingly recognized for their national security importance. As a result, information sharing and coordination between and among law enforcement and intelligence agencies have dramatically improved in recent years. Senior CIA officers serve at the FBI and vice versa. The intelligence community's Counter-Terrorism Center (CTC) is staffed by people drawn from a wide variety of intelligence and law enforcement agencies, and so is the FBI's Strategic Information Operations Center (SIOC), where terrorist and other threats are analyzed and responses coordinated. The CTC is headed by a CIA officer, with an FBI deputy; an FBI agent heads the SIOC, and his deputy comes from the CIA. There has also been broad interagency coordination, led by the NSC. An assistant-secretary level group, the Counterterrorism Security Group (CSG), which was chaired by a senior director at the NSC and later by the national coordinator for these issues, met frequently to coordinate U.S. counterterrorism policy.

Useful as these steps are, they do not go far enough. Interagency intelligence coordination should probably occur at a level one step higher than was the norm prior to September 11. Drawing on the Clinton administration's counterintelligence policy, which was finalized in the waning days of the administration,[31] a deputy-level coordinating committee should be set up. The committee should be chaired by Gen. Wayne Downing, the national director for combating terrorism and a deputy national security adviser, and should include deputies from the FBI, CIA, the departments of State, Justice, and Defense, and the Office of Homeland Security. The committee would meet regularly to recommend ways to improve coordination and to analyze information as required. A small, multiagency staff should support the committee and act as a direct liaison with the CTC and SIOC.

Finally, there may be scope for consolidating and rationalizing some of the federal law enforcement agencies.[32] Instead of many different investigative and enforcement agencies dealing with drugs, crime, terrorism, and the like, it may be useful to consolidate the dispersed investigative entities at the federal level (including the FBI, Drug Enforcement Agency, Bureau of Alcohol, Tobacco, and Firearms, the U.S. Secret Service, and others) into a Federal Investigative Agency, thus complementing the Federal Border Agency discussed above.

Department of Defense

Just days after the September 11 attack, the Pentagon released its quadrennial defense review declaring defense of the U.S. homeland to be "the Department's primary mission."[33] But reflecting America's historical invulnerability, its troops, forces, and organization have all been geared toward conducting operations overseas. There has been no Homeland Defense Command, nor is there a single person within the Office of the Secretary of Defense (OSD) in charge of homeland defense. The principal organizational issues for the Department of Defense are three: whether to create a single command for defense of the United States akin to the commands covering other regions of the globe; what role the National Guard should have in homeland defense; and whether there should be a high-level person within OSD responsible for coordinating Pentagon policy in this area.

The events of September 11 demonstrated that the Defense Department was not well prepared to deal with a major terrorist attack on U.S. soil. As Thomas White, the secretary of the Army, said later, "There was no unity of command in the traditional sense that, if we were in Afghanistan, we would have had Central Command in charge."[34] In early April 2002, Defense Secretary Donald Rumsfeld announced the creation of a new Northern Command to rectify this situation. This new command, which will commence on October 1, 2002, and be headed by a four-star general, will be in charge of all troops deployed as part of air patrols flying over the United States, naval vessels guarding the coasts, and emergency responses in case of a terrorist attack. It will absorb the North American Aerospace Defense Command, which has long been charged with overseeing defense of the United States and Canada against air and missile attacks. The new command will also take over control of the Joint Task Force Civil Support, which is responsible for assisting local first responders in case of a nuclear, chemical, or biological attack on U.S. territory. And it will be in charge of any U.S. military assistance in case of natural disasters such as hurricanes, floods, and forest fires. "This is the first time that the continental United States will be assigned a commander," Rumsfeld stated in making the announcement about the Northern Command. "The new commander will be responsible for land, aerospace, and sea defense of the United States. He will command U.S. forces that operate within the U.S. in support of civil authorities."[35] The creation of the Northern Command enjoys widespread, bipartisan support on Capitol Hill and is a useful step in streamlining the Defense Department's response to helping secure the American homeland against a terrorist attack.

There has been less attention so far to changing the role of the National Guard (see appendix E). Aside from conducting air patrols and standing guard at the nation's airports, the Pentagon has been extremely reluctant to employ National Guard forces in a homeland defense role. Requests by the Border Patrol and Customs Service for the temporary deployment of a few hundred National Guard troops while these agencies prepared to hire additional personnel were met with great hesitancy. Approval came only after weeks of careful deliberations, and then only with the clear understanding that their deployment would end by a date certain.[36] The reason for this reluctance is that while the Guard has responsibility for disaster and humanitarian relief as well as consequence management at the state level, it is today organized and equipped principally to support combat operations overseas. Together with the reserves, the National Guard has become the main backup of the regular armed forces. Therefore the military services see an expanding homeland defense role as a direct degradation of their combat capabilities abroad.

But if the Pentagon's primary mission is homeland defense, then it would make sense to assign as much of that responsibility as possible to the one military entity that is historically and constitutionally charged with that role—the National Guard. This will, admittedly, require a redistribution of resources, including combat support capabilities and material, to the reserves. But the Guard does not need tanks or artillery to defend against or respond to a terrorist attack. Instead, as the Hart-Rudman Commission rightly recommended, the National Guard should "provide a mobilization base with strong local ties and support," that could

—Participate in and initiate, where necessary, state, local, and regional planning for responding to a WMD incident; train and help organize local first responders.

—Maintain up-to-date inventories of military resources and equipment available in the area on short notice.

—Plan for rapid interstate support and reinforcement.

—Develop an overseas capability for international humanitarian assistance and disaster relief.[37]

One final Defense Department issue is the organization of the Office of the Secretary of Defense, the Pentagon's civilian and policy arm. Aside from a special assistant to the secretary of the army, who has a staff detailed from other parts of the Pentagon, there is no high-level civilian or policy official in charge of homeland defense today. In 2001 Secretary Rumsfeld requested congressional authorization to create two new under secretary posts within OSD, one for homeland security and another for intelligence. In addition to the new under secretary for homeland security, three new assistant secretaries would be established: for counterterrorism, support for civil authority, and for international and humanitarian support. The assistant secretary of defense for special operations and low-intensity conflict would also report to the new under secretary. Congress did not act on Rumsfeld's request and the secretary has now announced a plan to study the matter and come up with detailed recommendations by May 1, 2002.[38]

The decision to create a high-level policy position in the Pentagon responsible for homeland defense moves in the right direction. There must be a person accountable within this vast bureaucracy for what is now, after all, the department's self-described primary mission. Budgets, programs, and personnel decisions are more likely to reflect the importance of this mission if there are senior people responsible for making them. A new under secretary for homeland security supported by two, perhaps three, assistant secretaries would seem appropriate. The Pentagon and Congress should move swiftly to settle this matter.

Congress

However the executive branch conducts its work, many issues will inevitably engage the legislative branch. The president's ability to make homeland security his top priority will be helped, or hindered, according to whether and how much Congress can revamp its structure and process to the same end. Two reforms would be especially useful: establishment of House and Senate appropriations subcommittees for homeland security, and creation of a joint committee to oversee the national effort. The congressional role and focus would be further strengthened, moreover, if the Homeland Security Council were made a statutory entity, and its director subject to Senate confirmation—as recommended above.

One of Tom Ridge's signal achievements has been the submission of a unified homeland security budget. But once on Capitol Hill, it now must be disaggregated and its components distributed among multiple appropriations subcommittees. There they will be weighed not in relation to overall homeland security needs, but within such jurisdictions as Commerce, Justice, and State; Defense; and Labor, Health and Human Services, and Education. What the executive branch has laboriously pulled together, Congress must quickly pull apart. The obvious remedy, difficult though it may be to implement, is to establish new appropriations subcommittees on homeland security in both branches. If that proves too large a reform to swallow, a second-best alternative would be for the appropriations committees as a whole to take up and pass the homeland security budget.

Ideally, there would also be established authorizing committees with the same jurisdiction. In the near term, however, this would likely prove even harder to accomplish than appropriations reform. A useful "second-best" option, therefore, would be to enhance congressional capacity for analysis and oversight by creating a new body on the model of the Joint Economic Committee. This would limit the threat to existing jurisdictions, as a joint committee for homeland security would have no legislative authority. This would also limit its impact, of course, but such a committee could be a useful focal point, holding hearings, issuing reports, calling executive officials to task.

Summary and Conclusions

In terms of basic organization for homeland security, the Bush administration has made the best choice. There is greater potential for effective overall coordination and leadership in the new Homeland Security Council and Office than there would be in a new cabinet department, given the number of key functions that could *not* be included in such a department. Moreover,

Homeland Security Director Tom Ridge has moved effectively, for the most part, in building his organization and his role.

But as spelled out in this chapter, there is need for a number of additional steps:

—The Homeland Security Council should be made a statutory agency in the Executive Office of the President, with its director a cabinet-level official, subject to Senate confirmation.

—The HSC's strategic planning process should be reinforced through issuance of homeland security study directives on issues where the president must make fundamental policy and organizational choices. The options developed through the process would be debated at HSC meetings chaired by the president, who would then choose among them.

—Ridge's budgetary role should be strengthened by the creation of a new, dual-hatted position: senior director of OHS for budget policy and associate director of OMB for homeland security.

—A cadre of agency officials should be created that Ridge could deploy to the location of a terrorist incident to work with state and local officials and coordinate the federal government's response.

—A federal Border Agency should be established, comprising the Coast Guard, the Customs Service, the enforcement arm of the Immigration and Naturalization Service (including the Border Patrol), the Agriculture Quarantine Inspection program, and probably the new Transportation Security Agency.

—A deputy-level interagency committee, chaired by the NSC, should be created to coordinate information sharing and analysis among the intelligence and law enforcement committees.

—Under the secretary of defense, the decision to establish a new Northern Command to protect the homeland should be complemented by creation of a new post of under secretary for homeland security. The National Guard should return to its traditional, primary responsibility of homeland defense.

—Congress should establish appropriations subcommittees for homeland security, and a joint committee to exercise broad oversight in this area.

With reinforcing steps like these, and policy changes recommended in prior chapters, the United States will be better able to meet the daunting challenge of securing our homeland.[39]

8

CONCLUSION

The nation's response to the September 11 terrorist attacks has been energetic and impressive. From relief workers at home and abroad to military personnel in Afghanistan to those who lost family members in the attacks, Americans have shown courage and resolve. The Bush administration, the Congress, and countless state and local governments have taken urgent and major steps to reduce the country's vulnerability to further acts of terrorism.

Most homeland security steps to date, and the Bush administration's proposed budget for 2003, focus on preventing repeats of the September 11 attacks as well as the subsequent anthrax attacks and previous terrorist attacks against U.S. buildings or infrastructure or aircraft generally using conventional explosives. Primary focus has been placed on airline, airport, and airspace security, on preventing attacks against major infrastructure such as nuclear power plants and bridges and tunnels, on stockpiling vaccines and drugs to respond to biological agents, on trying to prevent suspected terrorists from entering and remaining in the United States, and on preventing terrorists from having easy access to financial resources here and overseas.

These steps have been important, but they are not comprehensive. The danger is that the nation will pursue a somewhat scattershot approach to countering terrorism without a broader strategic framework, unnecessarily imposing costs on the economy in exchange for limited reduction in the risk of attacks that could cause mass casualties or serious harm to our economy or society. It is important to focus systematically on priorities for countering a terrorist attack at its various stages. Excluding activities undertaken overseas, such as intelligence gathering (which is outside the scope of this volume), we propose a four-tier approach: first, to keep out dangerous people and objects before they can enter the country; second, to prevent terrorists from operating freely within the United States or from obtaining dangerous materials; third, to protect key sites that pose a risk of mass casualties or serious economic harm; and fourth, consequence management (reducing the toll from any attacks that still may occur).

First Tier: Perimeter Defense

Protecting the nation's borders against the entry of dangerous people and goods is the simplest objective to conceptualize. It means preventing terrorists or unregulated lethal materials from entering the nation in the first place. Three main types of entry are possible: by air, sea, or land. Most traffic would pass through airports, ports, road checkpoints, and railway lines. Undeveloped coastline and undeveloped border regions also need to be monitored, but even with these tasks added to the list, the challenge is easy to understand, even if somewhat less straightforward to address.

Some of the measures already adopted have helped to improve perimeter defense. For example, the nation has strengthened air security and immigration controls at border crossings since September 11. It has instituted new procedures governing ship traffic as well as truck traffic at border crossings. These steps respond to the obvious possibility of ships, airplanes, or vehicles being used either as transport for dangerous materials or people coming into the country or as weapons themselves.

But many other vulnerabilities remain within the category of perimeter security. Although airplanes are now being monitored much more carefully as they near and enter U.S. airspace, unmanned low-flying cruise missiles might well evade detection or interception. Although ships are being escorted into port when their crews are not well known or when their known cargoes are especially dangerous, the contents of container vessels are still being inspected only rarely.

Numerous vulnerabilities also exist in the way people enter the country, even after the steps taken since September 11. One important recent step: previously existing barriers between different intelligence and law enforcement agencies—the Central Intelligence Agency, Federal Bureau of Investigation, Federal Aviation Administration, Immigration and Naturalization Service, other U.S. agencies, their foreign counterparts, and their state and local counterparts here at home—are being broken down. In addition, databases of suspicious individuals or known terrorists are being integrated. But in many cases they do not yet operate in real time, due to hardware or software limitations, meaning that dangerous individuals cannot always be stopped as soon as they should be. Nor are databases comprehensive enough to ensure that suspicious individuals will be found quickly and apprehended if in the United States; and some enforcement agencies do not yet have access to each other's information.

Our proposals to improve perimeter defense (see chapter 2) would cost almost $10 billion a year, relative to the pre–September 11 budget plan for 2002.

Second Tier: Domestic Prevention

Not all threats are foreign, and not all foreign-based threats will be successfully stopped at U.S. borders. As a result, it is essential to take preventive steps domestically to monitor and apprehend would-be perpetrators before they can strike, as well as to restrict access to lethal materials and weapons.

Efforts must be made to track criminals, individuals overstaying visas, and suspected terrorists. We advocate a substantial increase in FBI counterterrorism staffing. In addition, databases connecting intelligence services with federal, state, and local law enforcement, immigration services, airline companies, universities, and other agencies and businesses must become much better integrated and more accessible operationally in real time, while taking care to avoid unnecessary intrusions into privacy. Some of these measures will follow naturally from those aimed at improving perimeter security, so in this sense there is considerable overlap between the first two of the otherwise largely separate lines of defense we propose for the United States.

More controversial are proposals for stepped-up monitoring, surveillance, and detection in the United States. Congress has already passed the USA Patriot Act, which expands and harmonizes intelligence authority across telecommunications modes, and also expands detection authority in the case of terrorism and related crime. Other measures could include standardized driver's licenses or national identity cards, perhaps with a biometric identifier.

It is also essential to secure dangerous materials. Among the most important are nuclear and biological materials, as well as large quantities of toxic chemicals and conventional explosives. More remains to be done here as well, particularly in the infrastructure for volatile and toxic chemicals. This infrastructure includes factories, pipelines, trucks, and storage sites. Guards have been increased and placed on higher alert at certain key locations; National Guard personnel have also been deployed. However, most such efforts have been directed to large facilities, and many chemical and natural gas facilities and some truck traffic are not yet carefully enough scrutinized, even though they are close to major cities.

Our proposals to bolster the nation's capacities to impede terrorists from operating in this country or gaining access to dangerous materials (see chapter 3) would cost almost $10 billion a year, again, relative to plans as they existed before September 11.

Third Tier: Protection of Critical Targets

Given the impossibility of protecting all sites against attack, policymakers should focus primarily on those that pose a risk of mass casualties or serious economic harm and on a small number of irreplaceable sites of national symbolic importance. The country's largest commercial and residential buildings, in which thousands of people live and work, remain vulnerable to attack. Efforts to prevent the release of weapons of mass destruction into air intake systems of buildings, subways, and stadiums have been meager to date. Similarly, large commercial buildings have not been adequately protected against truck bombs and fires. It is also important for the nation to defend its most prominent government buildings and national monuments, since a successful attack on them could embolden others to attack the United States and harm our sense of national self-confidence.

Protecting infrastructure is a particularly difficult task. Some infrastructure components are located at isolated, discrete sites and are therefore relatively straightforward, if not always easy, to protect: nuclear power plants and chemical plants, major bridges and tunnels, hospitals, stadiums, and subway lines. Other infrastructure is more dispersed or continuous; it includes rail lines, natural gas pipelines, FAA radar networks, water and electricity grids, banking networks, the postal system, and food distribution systems. Given the impossible task of protecting all such infrastructure, policymakers should concentrate on protecting against large-scale "single-node" failures, namely, those that would affect millions of people and impose large economic costs and could not be restored or replaced quickly.

The United States also remains too vulnerable to cyberattacks. Most such attacks would not directly cause many deaths, but they could badly disrupt the economy and indirectly kill people if hospitals, power plants, or other critical infrastructure were taken out of service for long periods. The disruption of telecommunications or vital cybersystems could be particularly dangerous if combined with other forms of attack, such as a chemical or biological attack.

Our proposals to protect key targets within the United States (see chapter 4) would cost about $10 billion a year, relative to pre–September 11 levels.

Fourth Tier: Consequence Management

Since perimeter defense, domestic prevention, and protection of key sites can all fail, it is also important to be able to mitigate the consequences of any attacks that should occur. The means must be available to treat rapidly victims of chemical or explosive attack (largely a job for first responders such as fire and police and emergency departments), to isolate and properly treat victims of biological attack (more a job for the public health and hospital system), and to detect biological attacks as soon as possible after they have begun (so that the number of individuals exposed to harmful agents can be minimized). Nunn-Lugar-Domenici funds have already started to make a significant difference in helping large cities prepare for possible attacks by chemical agents. But they are far from comprehensive in scope. Moreover, preparations for coping with a biological weapons attack, which are far different, have been less effective to date.

Our proposals for managing the consequences of a terrorist attack (see chapter 5) would cost almost $5 billion a year, roughly comparable to Bush administration plans for 2003.

The Administration's Budget Proposal

How does this approach compare in detail with the Bush administration's budget? The administration's 2003 proposal (see appendix B for further details) contains several priorities that are grouped into the following broad categories: supporting first responders, defending against biological terrorism, securing America's borders, using twenty-first century technology to defend the homeland, and aviation security. There are important similarities: "securing America's borders" is the same as our perimeter defense; "supporting first responders" is an element of consequence management, as are most of the measures proposed for defending against biological terrorism; "aviation security" is essentially a part of both perimeter security and protection against mass casualty attacks; and "cybersecurity and other twenty-first century technology" issues cut across our categories. Many of the specific proposals put forward by the Bush administration are similar to those advocated here.

Using our four-tier framework, however, helps identify some priority areas that the Bush administration did not emphasize in its budget. Within the area of perimeter security, its proposals for Customs and the Coast Guard are relatively modest in relation to the size of the unmet needs, as argued in chapter 2. They also appear to have some gaps in areas such as air defense. As for domestic prevention, the administration's plans are much less aggressive than ours in tracking terrorists and limiting access to dangerous materials. For example, we propose a much larger expansion in FBI staffing than the administration does and much more investment in information technology. In terms of protecting key sites, the Bush budget does little to improve the security of buildings against biological or conventional explosive attack. For consequence management, the administration's plans appear quite sufficient on the whole.

The broad program we propose thus overlaps considerably with the Bush administration plan. Indeed, perhaps two-thirds of our plan is similar to the administration's proposals. But the remaining one-third differs in important ways. By our estimates, even if the entire $38 billion Bush homeland security budget were implemented, between $5 billion and $10 billion in additional federal spending, as well as up to another $10 billion in private-sector spending, would still be needed each year to adopt measures that promise considerable security benefits for a modest cost. (We assume most investment costs would be made over a ten-year period, and so our estimates are for average annual costs over the next decade.) Specifically, we recommend the following:

—Major improvements and expansions in the Coast Guard and Customs Service, well beyond those already suggested by the Bush administration.

—Substantial expansions in domestic law enforcement agencies (again, well beyond those proposed by the Bush administration), in terms of personnel and information technology.

—Various measures for reducing the odds that biological agents could circulate through the air intake systems of major buildings and other large facilities.

—Enhancements in the nation's food safety programs.

—Additional measures for protecting buildings against conventional explosives and fires.

—Improved security measures for the nation's nuclear power plants and toxic chemical plants.

—A new approach to monitoring and protecting the nation's airspace.

—Numerous specific protective measures for other types of public and private infrastructure, including hazardous materials traffic and biological research centers.

Conclusion

The threat of future terrorist activity justifies a substantial investment by the nation in preventing such activity. The policies proposed here are intended to achieve significant risk reduction at reasonable economic and social costs. In addition to numerous specific steps, three broad strategies emphasized throughout the volume would help to improve the efficiency and reduce the economic consequences of protecting the homeland: the "EZ-pass" approach of providing some benefit (such as reduced waiting times or insurance premiums) to induce additional security precautions, having stakeholders pay for most security measures, and enhancing the use of modern information technologies to promote security.

Our proposals, in total, would cost the federal government about $45 billion a year, and the private sector up to $10 billion in all. Such costs are significant, but manageable. In its entirety, our proposed homeland security budget would total less than 15 percent of defense spending. Total defense and homeland security spending combined would remain about 4 percent of the gross domestic product (GDP), in contrast to defense spending levels during the Cold War, which were typically 5 to 10 percent of GDP. There are a number of alternative ways to pay for these costs without increasing the size of the deficit, including freezing some of the scheduled future tax cuts that were passed as part of the 2001 tax legislation or scaling back the proposed increase in defense spending.[1]

In summary, we believe the proposals in this volume would provide an effective and reasonably priced homeland security program. They would significantly reduce the risk of terrorism involving mass casualties, serious economic harm, or damage to key national symbols, without unduly impeding economic growth or the basic functioning of our society. As the nation's war on terrorism evolves, other steps may well be warranted, and some of the steps advocated here may become unnecessary. But the basic four-tier structure we propose for enhancing homeland security—defense of the nation's perimeter, preventive measures to track terrorists and secure dangerous materials, protection of domestic targets housing large numbers of people or representing a crucial part of our infrastructure, and the capacity to respond effectively to the consequences of a terrorist attack—should help to guide and focus policy decisions even as the most pressing needs within each category evolve.

THE LEGAL
LIABILITY SYSTEM

As noted in chapter 6, supporters of a voluntary approach to security measures may argue that the only required form of government intervention is the legal liability system, through which courts require actors held responsible for damages to others to provide compensation. One key question involving a liability approach is what standard of liability should apply: negligence or "strict liability"? Under a negligence standard, a firm is liable only if it is at fault; under strict liability, a firm can be liable even without a finding of fault. In the context of terrorist attacks, especially given the size of the potential damages and the presence of bankruptcy laws, it would appear to be infeasible—as well as inequitable—to hold firms or public entities strictly liable for all terrorism damage, even if constrained to damage that is reasonably foreseeable.[1]

A negligence standard, however, seems at least theoretically feasible: that is, parties could be held liable for negligence that allows terrorists to cause damage, and the knowledge of such liability could induce firms to undertake appropriate security measures. For example, the airlines whose airplanes were hijacked and flown into the World Trade Center could theoretically be held responsible for negligence in their airport screening.[2] But a negligence standard has its own implementation problems. One involves exactly what damages a negligence finding would cover. In the context of the airlines, would any negligence liability be limited to the losses of those who were killed on the planes, or would it extend to those who were killed and injured in the World Trade Center buildings (and to the owners of the buildings)? The reach of liability would presumably depend on the degree to which damages could have been reasonably foreseeable.

Although the foreseeability standard is a staple of legal textbooks, it can introduce substantial uncertainty in the terrorism context—which, as we will suggest shortly, can lead to socially suboptimal outcomes. Admittedly, once they are widely known, very specific dangers—such as the risk of contracting anthrax from the mail—are arguably foreseeable.[3] But even in these cases, what one jury in one jurisdiction may say constitutes negligence (assuming that is the liability standard) may not be the view of another jury, and vice versa. Much more problematic are the kinds of unexpected disasters, like those occurring on September 11, that have no precedent and, if they ever get to court, are judged by jury on first impression. To say the least, it is difficult, if not impossible, for private actors to anticipate these outcomes. All they can do is take "reasonable" precautions, but they have difficulty knowing with much precision what some jury will find to be reasonable several years after the fact. To the extent the courts provide little guidance, individuals and firms may be lulled into complacency and do very little to take precautions. On the other hand, large jury awards in some cases could induce the opposite behavior ("excessive deterrence"): the avoidance of otherwise socially desirable activities altogether, such as shutting down access to public spaces for extended periods of time.[4]

The fundamental problem is that a negligence approach requires some norm for the appropriate degree of precaution; only if firms or individuals fail to meet that norm are they found to be negligent. To be sure, a government regulatory standard could establish the norm, and courts could rely on the mandate as implicitly defining an appropriate degree of precaution. But in other contexts, meeting a regulatory standard has not always proved to be a sufficient defense. In any event, in the absence of explicit regulatory guidance, what is reasonable behavior must be decided on a case-by-case basis. Given the lack of direct precedents for determining negligence and the possibility that terrorist attacks will be relatively infrequent, the case law in this area may be slow to develop. In the meanwhile, firms would be unsure of what levels of care they must exercise in order to avoid a finding of negligence.

Therefore relying solely on the liability system, even if negligence is the operative standard, could prove to be inefficient and excessively costly, as firms eschew certain activities because of uncertainties introduced by potentially different jury decisions. A more direct form of government intervention is more appropriate.

APPENDIX

B

THE BUSH HOMELAND
SECURITY BUDGET

On February 4, 2002, Director Tom Ridge of the White House
Office of Homeland Security unveiled his proposed budget for
homeland security for 2003. It began by defining a homeland
security budget for the first time. Under previous administra-
tions, no such unified budget had existed. In recent years, budget
categories were created to capture counterterrorist spending and
the protection of critical infrastructure, but these categories did
not include most efforts of agencies such as the Coast Guard and
several others that have obvious homeland security ramifications.

Using the new homeland security budget concept reveals how
quickly spending in this area has been rising in recent years. In
fact, the increases began well before September 11. In 1995 the
estimated spending for homeland security was $9.0 billion; by
2000 it was $13.2 billion; in 2001 it was $16.9 billion (the last $0.9
being added after September 11).

Moving to 2002, the federal government's planned homeland
security budget would have been about $19.5 billion prior to the
September 11 attacks; after the hijackings, about $9.8 billion
more was added in a supplemental appropriation, making for a
total of $29.3 billion, and another $5.2 billion has since been

Table B-1. *Homeland Security Funding by Initiative Area*

Millions of dollars, fiscal years

Initiative	2002 enacted base	First 2002 supple- mental	Second 2002 supplemental (proposed March 2002)	2003 Bush admin- istration proposal
Supporting first responder/ crisis management	291	651	350	3,500
Defending against biological terrorism	1,408	3,730	100	5,898
Securing America's borders	8,752	1,194	290	10,615
Using twenty-first century technology to defend the homeland	155	75	50	722
Aviation security	1,543	1,035	4,300	4,800
Other non-Department of Defense homeland security	3,186	2,384	100	5,352
Department of Defense homeland security (outside initiatives)	4,201	689	0	6,815
Total	19,535	9,758	5,200	37,702

Source: *Securing the Homeland and Strengthening the Budget,* February, 2002 (www.white-house.gov/homeland/homeland_security_book.pdf).

Note: Assuming passage of the March 2002 supplemental funding request, the 2002 total will be $34.5 billion. The breakdown of the $5.2 billion supplemental request by category is approximate.

requested as a supplemental appropriation. For 2003, Governor Ridge is proposing a total of $37.7 billion, or roughly twice the original 2002 plan, and four times what the government was spending on homeland security in the mid-1990s.

As noted in chapter 8, Director Ridge's budget plan for 2003 usefully contained several priority areas that can be grouped into broad conceptual categories (see table B-1 for the proposed increases in spending by category): supporting first responders, defending against biological terrorism, securing America's borders, using twenty-first century technology to defend the homeland, and aviation security.

Table B-2. *Supporting First Responders through the Federal Emergency Management Agency and the Department of Justice*
Millions of dollars, fiscal years[a]

Activity[b]	2002 enacted base	2002 supplemental	2003 proposed[c]
Equip first responder team	159	188	770
Train state and local first responders	56	171	665
Assist emergency response planning	3	24	35
Enhance communications infrastructure to support interoperability	0	113	1,365
Improve command and control to ensure effective procedures at response sites	0	17	35
Fund interjurisdictional agreements and mutual aid compacts	0	0	140
Disseminate information regarding emergency response to the public	0	0	135
Provide federal technical assistance to state and local emergency response agencies	36	30	350
Test readiness and provide feedback on performance	7	85	105
Other	30	25	0
Total, first responders	291	651	3,500

Source: *Securing the Homeland and Strengthening the Budget*, February, 2002 (www.white-house.gov/homeland/homeland_security_book.pdf).

a. Proposed allocations by activity reflect approximate percentage allocations with adjustments where funding was for mixed activities or not provided.

b. Funds for fiscal 2002 represent funding for both FEMA ($39 million base and no funds in the supplemental) and Justice ($252 million base and $651 million in the supplemental).

c. The proposal for fiscal 2003 provides state and local governments flexibility to target funds to their needs. All funds for fiscal 2003 are requested for FEMA.

FIRST RESPONDERS. The budget for supporting first responders would grow by $3.2 billion over the initial 2002 budget (or $2.5 billion over the actual 2002 budget reflecting supplemental appropriations as well). It would be used primarily for equipment, training, and communications infrastructure for the nation's 2 million police, fire, and emergency medical personnel. In many ways, it is the logical successor to the much smaller Nunn-Lugar-Domenici program, launched in the mid-1990s. These funds focus more on responses to chemical, conventional, or nuclear devices than to biological agents, where victims would generally first show up in hospitals rather than the actual site of an attack.

BIOLOGICAL TERRORISM. The budget would increase by $4.5 billion over the initial 2002 budget plan. This would only be $800 million higher than the revised 2002 budget, but that budget included large one-time costs for purchasing smallpox vaccine and pharmaceuticals and decontaminating postal facilities. Those expenses are not expected to recur, so in fact, the 2003 budget contains substantial funds for new initiatives. Most of the increase is in the area of research and development for defenses, medications, and detectors and will go toward work performed by the National Institutes of Health, the Centers for Disease Control, the Food and Drug Administration, and the Department of Defense. Smaller increases are proposed for medical surveillance and communications (about $300 million), and for public health and hospital infrastructure (about $200 million).

An increase of about $1.9 billion over the original 2002 budget is being requested for border security (an increase of $700 million over the post-September 11 budget for 2002). The major increases are for agencies such as the Department of Justice's Border Patrol agency, Treasury's Customs, and the Department of Transportation's Coast Guard.

TWENTY-FIRST CENTURY TECHNOLOGY. Most of the funding in this category is related to information technology. The increase would total $600 million over the original 2002 budget, and about $500 million over the post-September 11 budget. About $100 million is for cyberspace protection; the bulk of the funds are proposed for an entry-exit visa system to keep better track of foreigners inside the United States (nearly $400 million).

AVIATION SECURITY. The proposed funding amounts to $4.8 billion in 2003, a tripling of the initial 2002 budget and an increase of $2.2 billion even taking into account the post-September 11 supplemental appropriations. Most of the added spending on airports and airlines was made necessary by legislation passed in the fall of 2001; the 2003 budget would include large increases to fund measures that have already been widely debated and mandated.

Table B-3. *Securing America's Borders*
Millions of dollars, fiscal years

Activity	2002 enacted base	2002 supplemental	2003 proposed
Immigration and Naturalization Service (Justice): Enforcement[a]	4,111	570	4,963
Select components:			
Border Patrol	1,256	68	1,471
Inspections	821	125	999
Detention and deportation	1,029	10	1,100
Unspecified emergency response requirements (supplemental funding only)		72	
Entry-exit visa system (non-add)	17	13	380
INS including entry-exit visa system	4,128	583	5,343
United States Customs Service (Treasury): Inspections	1,713	364	2,332
Select components:			
Northern border security	532	117	744
Customs maritime security	355	109	684
United States Coast Guard (Transportation): Enforcement	2,631	209	2,913
Select components:			
Ports, waterways, and coastal security	473	209	1,213
Interdiction activities	778	0	587
Capital programs	636	0	725
Animal and Plant Health Inspection Service (USDA): Agricultural Quarantine Program, border inspections	297	50	407
Total, border security	8,752	1,194	10,615
Total including entry-exit visa system	8,769	1,207	10,995

Source: *Securing the Homeland and Strengthening the Budget,* February, 2002 (www.white-house.gov/homeland/homeland_security_book.pdf).

a. Fiscal 2003 figure includes $615 million proposed to be transferred to the detention trustee.

Table B-4. *Defending against Biological Terrorism*[a]

Millions of dollars, fiscal years

Activity	2002 enacted base	2002 supplemental	2003 proposed
Enhance medical communications and surveillance capabilities			
Information/communications systems	34	40	202
Medical surveillance systems	0	0	175
Epidemiologist exchange program	0	0	10
Media/public information campaign	0	0	5
Total	34	40	392
Strengthen state and local health systems[b]			
Hospital infrastructure (labs and decon)	0	0	283
State public health lab capacity	13	15	200
Hospital mutual aid (planning/coordination)	5	135	235
State epidemiological teams	0	0	80
Educational incentives for curriculum	0	0	60
Hospital training exercises with states	0	0	73
Public health preparedness planning	29	810	210
Metropolitan medical response system (MMRS)	20	0	60
Total	67	960	1,202
Research and development			
Basic and applied biodefense research (NIH)	93	85	1,080
Biodefense research infrastructure (NIH)	0	70	336
Anthrax vaccine development (NIH and CDC)	18	0	268
Expedited drug approval/research (FDA)	7	41	49
Research facility security upgrades (HHS)	0	84	100
Bioweapons defense/countermeasures (DOD)			120
Agent identification, detection, and area monitoring (DOD)			300
Other research and development (DOD)	182	1	182
Total	300	281	2,435

Table B-4. (*continued*)

Activity	*2002 enacted base*	*2002 supplemental*	*2003 proposed*
Improve federal response			
National pharmaceutical stockpile	52	593	300
Upgrade CDC capacity and labs, including BL 4 Lab	18	60	109
Fort Collins (HHS)	0	0	100
Improving decontamination methods (EPA)	0	0	75
Federal public health response teams	6	45	43
Federal preparedness planning	0	0	10
Total	76	698	637
Other bioterrorism preparedness			
Smallpox vaccine purchase	0	512	100
Food safety (FDA)	0	97	99
Rapid toxic screening (HHS)	5	10	15
Other HHS	43	40	118
Drinking water safety (EPA)	2	88	22
Postal Service decontamination	0	675	0
Procurement of biodefense equipment and counterproliferation (DOD)	337	63	337
Other agencies and activities	544	266	542
Total, bioterrorism	**1,408**	**3,730**	**5,898**

Source: *Securing the Homeland and Strengthening the Budget,* February, 2002 (www.white-house.gov/homeland/homeland_security_book.pdf).

a. Does not include funding in the First Responder initiative.

b. Total for state and local assistance in FY 2003 is $ 1.6 billion, which includes funding for communications/ surveillance systems, and to assist state and local receipt and delivery of national pharmaceutical stockpile supplies.

Table B-5. *Using 21st-Century Technology to Defend the Homeland*
Millions of dollars, fiscal years

Measure	2002 enacted base	2002 supplemental	2003 proposed
Assure broad access and horizontal sharing across selected federal databases:			
Program Office to identify and commence process for information sharing (Commerce)	0	0	20
Ensure procedures for and handling of sensitive homeland security information to facilitate information sharing while protecting sources:			
Secure videoconferencing with states (Federal Emergency Management Agency)[a]	0	0	7
Entry-exit visa system (also represented as a non-add to the Border Initiative-funding to Immigration and Naturalization Service)	17	13	380
Assure relevant information about threats is conveyed to state and local officials in a timely manner:	3	0	17
Threat dissemination systems (Justice)	3	0	10
Educational program for state and local officials (National Archives and Records Administration)	0	0	7
Cyberspace security—protecting our information infrastructure:	135	62	298
National Infrastructure Simulation and Analysis Center (Energy)[b]	0	0	20
Cyber Warning Intelligence Network (Defense)	0	0	30
Priority Wireless Access (Defense)	0	0	60
GovNet Feasibility Study (General Services Administration)	0	0	5
Cybercorps (National Science Foundation)	11	0	11
Federal Computer Incident Response Capability (General Services Administration)	10	0	11
National Infrastructure Protection Center (NIPC) (FBI)	72	61	126
Computer Security Division (NIST)	11	0	15
Critical Infrastructure Assurance Office (Commerce)	5	1	7
Other IT/information sharing	26	0	15
Total, IT/information sharing	155	75	722

Source: *Securing the Homeland and Strengthening the Budget,* February, 2002 (www.whitehouse.gov/homeland/homeland_security_book.pdf).

a. Includes funding under the First Responder Initiative.

b. Does not include $20 million in supplemental funding provided to Defense for the NISAC. Funds are included in the Defense total.

Figure B-1. *Homeland Security Distribution of Fiscal 2003 Request by Agency*

Billions of dollars

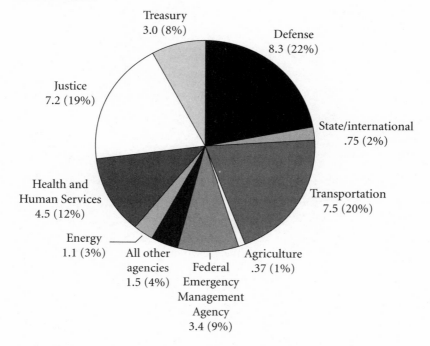

Treasury
3.0 (8%)

Defense
8.3 (22%)

Justice
7.2 (19%)

State/international
.75 (2%)

Health and
Human Services
4.5 (12%)

Transportation
7.5 (20%)

Energy
1.1 (3%)

All other
agencies
1.5 (4%)

Federal
Emergency
Management
Agency
3.4 (9%)

Agriculture
.37 (1%)

Source: *Securing the Homeland and Strengthening the Budget,* February, 2002 (www.whitehouse gov/homeland/homeland_security_book.pdf).

APPENDIX

C

FUNDING TO COMBAT
TERRORISM, PAST AND FUTURE

Table C-1. *Appropriations for Combating Terrorism and Protecting Critical Infrastructure since 1998 and the Funding Requested for 2002 before September 11, 2001*
Millions of dollars

Department or agency	1998	1999	2000	President's request for	
				2001	2002
Defense and intelligence agencies	4,919	5,485	6,757	7,267	8,252[a]
State	202	1,654	792	1,311	1,549
Justice	630	716	765	939	1,038
Energy	505	619	724	754	834
Treasury	401	423	406	475	474
Health and Human Services	53	218	325	387	446
Transportation	192	296	313	366	401
All others	295	385	372	537	573
Total budgetary authority[b]	7,197	9,794	10,454	12,036	13,566

Source: Congressional Budget Office (CBO) based on Office of Management and Budget, *Annual Report to Congress on Combating Terrorism* (July 2001) (www.cbo.gov/showdoc.cfm?index=3277&sequence=8).

a. This figure for the Department of Defense and intelligence agencies is different from the one in the Office of Management and Budget's report because CBO has included an adjustment made in the president's fiscal 2002 amended budget request.

b. The totals shown here are larger than those presented by the Congressional Research Service and other organizations because CBO has included funds for protecting critical infrastructure.

Table C-2. *Estimated 2002 Funding for Combating Terrorism and Protecting Critical Infrastructure, by Office of Management and Budget's Classification of Purpose*[a]

Millions of dollars

Department or agency	Law enforcement and investigative	Research and development	Preparing for and responding to terrorist acts	President's request for physical security of national populace	Physical security of government	Critical infrastructure protection	Total
Defense and intelligence agencies	2,888	303	735	41	3,498	1,850	9,314
Health and Human Services	97	294	2,485	0	94	98	3,067
Justice	1,330	24	987	0	227	66	2,633
State	77	6	7	0	1,427	32	1,549
Transportation	7	101	22	804	13	412	1,360
Energy	1	134	45	1	834	50	1,065
Treasury	292	1	35	65	234	84	711
Agriculture	12	102	51	0	174	2	341
Federal Emergency Management Agency	0	0	277	0	2	2	281
Postal Service	0	0	0	250	0	0	250
Legislative Branch	0	0	0	0	232	0	232
National Air and Space Administration	0	0	0	0	89	137	226
General Services Administration	14	0	2	0	185	10	210
District of Columbia	0	0	135	39	26	0	200
Interior	5	0	1	2	89	32	128
Judiciary	0	0	0	0	105	0	105
Social Security Administration	0	0	0	0	4	101	105
Environmental Protection Agency	0	8	8	39	36	2	93
Commerce	12	4	0	0	13	42	71
Executive Office of the President	0	0	17	0	8	25	50
Veterans Affairs	0	0	0	0	2	22	24
Labor	0	0	0	0	0	23	23
International assistance	0	0	1	0	11	0	12
Education	0	0	0	0	0	9	9
Other independent agencies	2	0	0	4	3	175	185

Table C-2. *(continued)*

Department or agency	Law enforce- ment and investi- gative	Research and develop- ment	Preparing for and respond- ing to terror- ist acts	President's request for physical secur- ity of national populace	Physical secur- ity of govern- ment	Critical infra- structure protec- tion	Total
Total budget authority	4,737	977	4,807	1,245	7,305	3,172	22,242
Percentage of total budget authority	21	4	22	6	33	14	100
Memorandum: President's request for 2002	3,694	511	864	283	5,726	2,488	13,566
Amounts added after September 11	1,043	466	3,943	962	1,578	684	8,676[b]

Source: Congressional Budget Office based on Office of Management and Budget, *Annual Report to Congress on Combating Terrorism* (July 2001) (www.cbo.gov/showdoc.cfm?index=3277&sequence=8).

a. These figures include funds associated with combating terrorism and protecting critical infrastructure according to OMB's classifications in its July 2001 report. They exclude an estimated $1.25 billion authorized by P.L. 107-71 for aviation security, which is to be offset by fees. They also exclude certain other "homeland security" budget items.

b. Of the roughly $8.7 billion in added funds for 2002, about $8 billion was from emergency supplemental legislation (P.L. 107-117), and about $700 million was added in the 13 regular appropriation acts, according to CBO's estimates.

Table C-3. *Dispersal of Second $20 Billion Supplemental, Fall 2001 (for Fiscal 2002)*
Billions of dollars

Category	Second dispersal	Total (including first dispersal)
Defense	3.5	17.2
Reconstruction/relief	8.2	11.1
Homeland defense	8.3	9.9

Source: Senate Appropriations Committee Chairman Robert Byrd, December 18, 2001 (http://appropriations.senate.gov/releases/record.cfm?id=180061).

THE COAST GUARD

Table D-1. *Essential Coast Guard Services, 1999*

Coast Guard missions	Coast Guard successes
Maritime safety	The Coast Guard Saved approximately 3,800 lives, conducted 141,000 courtesy maritime examinations on pleasure craft, taught 211,000 recreational sailors the rules of the sea and performed more than 50,000 inspections on merchant vessels.
Maritime security	The Coast Guard also prevented 111,689 pounds of cocaine, 28,872 pounds of marijuana, and 32,634 pounds of hashish from entering the United States. In addition the Coast Guard interdicted 4,333 illegal immigrants.
Protection of natural resources	The Coast Guard boarded over 15,000 fishing vessels to check for compliance with safety and environmental laws, conducted 900 inspections of offshore drilling units, and responded to 12,500 reports of water pollution or hazardous material releases.
Maritime mobility	In addition, the Coast Guard ensured the safe passage of one million commercial vessel transits through congested harbors with Vessel Traffic Services while maintaining more than 50,000 aids to navigation, including 15,000 along 11,900 miles of navigable rivers.
National defense	Finally, the Coast Guard sent International Training Teams to help more than 50 countries develop their maritime services. They also interdicted oil illegally being smuggled out of Iraq.

Source: *U.S. Coast Guard Fiscal Year 2001 Budget in Brief.*
Note: Many of these activities were at least temporarily curtailed after September 11.

Figure D-1. *Coast Guard Assets*

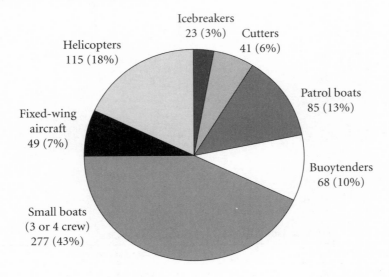

Source: *U.S. Coast Guard Fiscal Year 2001 Budget in Brief,* U.S. Coast Guard, 2000.

Figure D-2. *Coast Guard Operating Expenses Budget by Program*

Millions of dollars

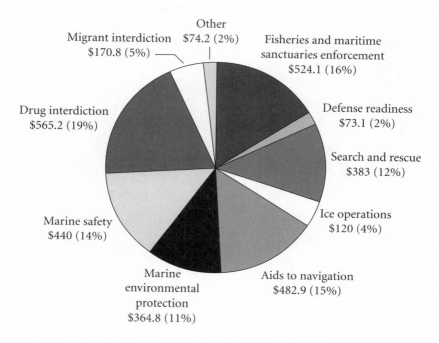

Source: *U.S. Coast Guard Fiscal Year 2001 Budget in Brief,* U.S. Coast Guard, 2000.

E

THE NATIONAL GUARD

President Bush called up the National Guard under Title 10. Guard members are helping support our mission abroad and are under federal jurisdiction. Many are still in the states, but they are training, or mobilizing or acting in support of the mission in Afghanistan.

The Guard has been called up under three different jurisdictions:

—President Bush asked governors to call up the Guard to protect airports under Title 32. These call-ups are the governors' responsibilities, but the federal government is committed to paying the states for this duty.

—Governors have called up the Guard on their own accord for the purpose of protecting other critical facilities or doubling as law enforcement. This is independent of the federal government programs.

—Normal Duty Reserves are those who fulfill Noble Eagle/Enduring Freedom missions although they were not called up for that purpose. For example, training missions often double as air patrol support. These are Guard and service people who would have been on duty regardless of the events following September 11.

Table E-1. *Guard and Reserve Components of Homeland Security and Antiterror Foreign Operations*
Number of personnel

	Service mission and status					
	Enduring Freedom/ Noble Eagle		*Airport security and site protection*[a]	*Site protection and law enforce-ment*	*Enduring Freedom/ Noble Eagle*	
Service	*Mobilized under 12302*	*Temporary tour of active duty*	*Title 32 (active) duty for special work)*	*State duty (volunteer)*	*Normal duty reserves and guard*	*Totals*
Army National Guard	15,713	49	5,765	1,373	1,634	24,534
Air National Guard	12,053	0	467	5	673	13,198
Army Reserve	17,623	0	0	0	6,514	24,137
Air Force Reserve	12,822	0	0	0	1,471	14,293
Naval Reserve	9,164	0	0	0	20	9,184
Marine Corps Reserve	4,387	0	0	0	41	4,428
Coast Guard Reserve	1,789	0	0	0	36	1,825
Total	73,551	49	6,232	1,378	10,389	91,599

Source: Media Relations, National Guard Bureau Public Affairs Office, November 14, 2001, and April 22, 2002.

a. Only the National Guard can fulfill these duties. Reserve forces are prohibited from engaging in domestic law enforcement efforts by constitutional constraints. Force protection includes activities such as guard duty at government facilities or infrastructure. Forces are guarding borders, nuclear facilities, bridges, state building, and ports. In addition, Guard members are working in WMD/NBC detection and are assisting the Capitol Police in the District of Columbia in the protection of federal buildings.

NOTES

Chapter 1

1. As explained in chapter 6, the costs related to terrorist attacks consist of the direct loss of physical and human capital as a result of the attack, and the macroeconomic costs caused by the interruption to normal American life and business activities. According to current estimates, insured losses from the attacks—which provide a proxy for the direct loss of physical and human capital—may amount to between $36 billion and $54 billion. Moreover, if half the difference between actual GDP growth after September 11 and previously projected growth is attributed to the attacks, losses from reduced economic activity amounted to about $50 billion, making for a total loss of about $100 billion.

2. For a related taxonomy, see Kurt M. Campbell and Michele A. Flournoy, *To Prevail: An American Strategy for the Campaign against Terrorism* (Washington: CSIS, 2001), pp. 105–21. See also Ashton B. Carter, "The Architecture of Government in the Face of Terrorism," *International Security* (Winter 2001/02), pp. 5–23.

3. For a similar view, see Anthony H. Cordesman, *Terrorism, Asymmetric Warfare, and Weapons of Mass Destruction: Defending the U.S. Homeland* (Westport, Conn.: Praeger, 2002), pp. 1–11.

4. Carter, "The Architecture of Government in the Face of Terrorism," pp. 17–18.

5. This should be an ongoing effort, though the details are likely to be classified so as not to provide a road map to terrorists as to what is protected and what is not.

6. This accounting follows that proposed by the Bush administration. See Office of Homeland Security, "Securing the Homeland, Strengthening the Nation," The White House, Washington, February 2002 [www.whitehouse.gov/homeland_security_book.pdf].

7. For further discussion of this idea, see William G. Gale and Peter R. Orszag, "Keep Existing Tax Cuts but Freeze New Ones," *Los Angeles Times*, January 28, 2002; and Peter R. Orszag, *The Budget and the Economy*, Testimony before the U.S. Senate Budget Committee, January 29, 2002.

8. The federal government heavily subsidized the hiring of local community law enforcement officers through several programs under the Office of Community Oriented Policing Services (COPS), but the motivation for that initiative was not related to homeland security.

Chapter 2

1. Another "point of entry" into the country is the Internet. A cyberattack can be launched from abroad and impose substantial economic and social costs on the United States by bringing down or corrupting computer systems that control vital infrastructure or that play a central role in the national economy. However, because the steps required to protect U.S. computer systems against attack from abroad are similar (and often identical) to those required to protect the systems against attack from domestic locations, we address cybersecurity issues in chapter 4, on internal defense.

2. See, for example, Michael Grunwald, "Economic Crossroads on the Line: Security Fears Have U.S. and Canada Rethinking Life at 49th Parallel," *Washington Post*, December 26, 2001, p. A01.

3. For a recent analysis of this topic, see James M. Lindsay and Michael E. O'Hanlon, *Defending America: The Case for Limited National Defense* (Brookings, 2001). It advocates a limited, two-tier defense that would cost some $40 billion to develop and deploy.

4. Testimony of Secretary of Defense Donald Rumsfeld and Chairman of the Joint Chiefs of Staff General Richard Myers, *Fiscal Year 2003 Department of Defense Budget*, Hearing before the Senate Committee on Armed Services, 107 Cong. 2 sess. (February 5, 2002), p. 11 [www.defenselink.mil/speeches/2002/s20020205-secdef2.html].

5. Dave Moniz, "Fewer Jet Patrols over U.S. Sought," *USA Today*, January 15, 2002, p. 1.

6. The states include Alaska, Hawaii, Massachusetts, New York, Pennsylvania, New Jersey, Virginia, both Carolinas, northern and southern and western Florida, Alabama, Louisiana, New Mexico, Arizona, southern California, Oregon, Idaho,

North Dakota, Minnesota, Wisconsin, Michigan, and Ohio (as well as many interior states, of course).

7. William B. Scott, "Domestic Air Patrols Tax Tankers, AWACS," *Aviation Week and Space Technology*, October 8, 2001, p. 68; Bradley Graham, "Eagle Eyes over the Homeland," *Washington Post*, October 30, 2001, p. 1.

8. Bradley Graham and Bill Miller, "Pentagon Debates Homeland Defense Role," *Washington Post*, February 11, 2002, p. 6.

9. The Air National Guard has been flying about 80 percent of the continental air defense missions since September 11; see Graham, "Eagle Eyes over the Homeland," p. 1.

10. Response of General Ralph Eberhart, Commander in Chief, U.S. Space Command, *Role of the Department of Defense in Homeland Security*, Hearing before the Senate Armed Services Committee, 107 Cong. 1 sess. (October 25, 2001), p. 17.

11. For other comments on the possible need for cruise missile defense, see Heritage Foundation Homeland Security Task Force, *Defending the American Homeland* (Washington: Heritage Foundation, 2002), p. 9.

12. The radar horizon, measured in miles, is roughly equal to the square root of twice an object's height, measured in feet. In other words, an object at an altitude of 50 feet could be seen at a distance of 10 miles, since 2 x 50 = 100, and the square root of 100 is 10. See J. C. Toomay, *Radar Principles for the Non-Specialist*, 2d ed. (Mendham, N.J.: Scitech, 1989), pp. 160–61.

13. Short-range missiles would typically cost perhaps $1 million to $3 million apiece; their associated ground installations would add to that tab. If 10 were based at each of 100 locations, total acquisition costs for the missiles and their ground support might be $5 billion to $10 billion. Radar based in the air might cost anywhere from several tens of millions to several hundred million each, depending on their sophistication and on how successful engineers may be at finding inexpensive solutions. If 100 were needed at $100 million each, they would cost $10 billion. If, by contrast, costs could be held to those for advanced unmanned aerial vehicles (UAVs) such as the Global Hawk, the airframe's unit cost might decline in half (though the radar would be additional). Furthermore, given the long endurance of that aircraft, fewer total aircraft might be needed to keep a certain number in the sky at a time, so total acquisition costs for the airborne platforms might be held to under $5 billion. Operating costs would, of course, be extra. For a UAV, annual operating costs might be $3 million to $5 million. For a medium-sized aircraft, costs would more likely be $5 million to $10 million each year. Assuming roughly 100 such aircraft, annual costs would thus be $300 million to $1 billion, depending on the capabilities of the airframe and the radar.

14. The above numbers ignore several other factors that could change costs significantly. However, two of them would tend to raise costs, and the others would tend to lower them, so the net effect would likely be quite modest, and the above estimates might turn out to be reasonably accurate. One factor that would raise

costs would be the need for command, control, and battle management infrastructure to connect radars to each other and to interceptors. As one guidepost to possible costs, command and communications facilities for the proposed midcourse ballistic missile defense system designed by the Clinton administration were expected to cost just over $2 billion (or about 10 percent of the total). In addition, costs of $1.5 billion were expected for construction of major sites; similar demands would arise for the above cruise missile defense. Lower costs would likely result from the fact that existing Federal Aviation Administration radar might make it unnecessary to purchase and deploy radar in some parts of U.S. coastal regions. In addition, as already noted, aerostat balloons with very long endurance might be able to replace ground radars in a number of locations at considerably lower cost.

15. Assistant Commandant, Operations, U.S. Coast Guard, *America's Coast Guard* (Washington: Department of Transportation, 2000), pp. 83–92.

16. U.S. Coast Guard, *Coast Guard Fiscal Year 2001 Agency Capital Plan* (Washington: Department of Transportation, 2000), pp. 20–21.

17. Jack Dorsey, "Coast Guard Prepares to Initiate Deep Cuts," *Norfolk Virginia-Pilot*, April 24, 2001.

18. Mortimer L. Downey, ed., *Report of the Interagency Task Force on U.S. Coast Guard Roles and Missions* (Washington: Department of Transportation, 1999), pp. 2–39.

19. Statement of Admiral James M. Loy, Commandant, U.S. Coast Guard, Hearing before the Coast Guard and Maritime Transportation Subcommittee of the House Transportation and Infrastructure Committee, 107 Cong. 2 sess. (December 6, 2001), p. 23.

20. See Eric Pianin and Bradley Graham, "At Home and Abroad, Security Is Stepped Up," *Washington Post*, October 8, 2001, p. A3; Randal C. Archibold, "Coast Guard Will Not End Boat Patrols Near A-Plants," *New York Times*, October 20, 2001; Edward Walsh, "For Coast Guard, Priorities Shifted on September 11," *Washington Post*, November 26, 2001, p. A23.

21. Loy, Hearing (December 6, 2001), p. 23. Each unit has a core of 8 to 10 active-duty personnel and about 120 reservists (p. 29).

22. Ibid., p. 23.

23. Walsh, "For Coast Guard, Priorities Shifted on September 11," p. A23.

24. Response of Secretary of Transportation Norman Mineta, Hearing before the Coast Guard and Maritime Transportation Subcommittee of the House Transportation and Infrastructure Committee, 107 Cong. 1 sess. (December 6, 2001), p. 16; Jack Dorsey, "Navy Gives Patrol Craft to Coast Guard for Use," *Virginian-Pilot*, January 10, 2002.

25. Testimony of Admiral James M. Loy, Commandant, U.S. Coast Guard, Hearing before the Transportation Subcommittee of the Senate Commerce Committee (October 11, 2001); Walsh, "For Coast Guard, Priorities Shifted on September 11," p. A23.

26. Loy, Hearing (October 11, 2001).

27. Mineta,Hearing.

28. Loy, Hearing (December 6, 2001), p. 26.

29. Gregory J. Sanial, "National Security Depends on Deepwater," *Proceedings* (November 2001), pp. 76–79.

30. Since an average small vessel might cost $1 million to $2 million to buy and $2 million to $5 million to operate over a lifetime of 30 to 40 years, annual costs would have to go up by $1 billion or so for this category of Coast Guard assets. Personal communication from Roy Nash, U.S. Coast Guard, November 2001.

31. Loy, Hearing (December 6, 2001), p. 27; *Bus and Truck Security and Hazardous Materials Licensing,* Hearing before the Surface Transportation and Merchant Marine Subcommittee of the Senate Commerce Committee, 107 Cong. 1 sess. (October 10, 2001), p. 44.

32. Graham Allison, "Could Worse Be Yet to Come?" *Economist,* November 1, 2001.

33. Mineta, Hearing, p. 20.

34. Stephen Flynn, "Beyond Border Control," *Foreign Affairs,* November/ December 2000.

35. See "Security as a Trade Barrier," *Business Week,* December 31, 2001; and David Hummels, "Time as a Trade Barrier," Purdue University (October 2000).

36. Flynn, "Beyond Border Control."

37. Robert C. Bonner, "The Customs Patrol," *Washington Post,* February 16, 2002.

38. Loy, Hearing (December 6, 2001), p. 27.

39. *Bus and Truck Security and Hazardous Materials Licensing,* Hearing, p. 34.

40. Congressional Budget Office, Cost Estimate for S. 1214, Port and Maritime Security Act of 2001, September 18, 2001.

41. Flynn, "Beyond Border Control," p. 57.

42. Tim Weiner, "U.S. and Mexico to Share Work at the Border," *New York Times,* March 6, 2002, p. A8.

43. Whether and in what way we should expand foreign intelligence collection on possible terrorists is beyond the scope of this study; for domestic intelligence, see chapter 3.

44. Statement of Mary Ryan, *Technology's Role in Preventing the Entry of Terrorists into the United States,* Hearing before the Senate Judiciary Subcommittee on Technology, Terrorism, and Government Information, 107 Cong. 1 sess. (October 12, 2001).

45. Ibid.

46. General Accounting Office, *Major Management Challenges and Program Risks: Department of State,* GAO-01-252 (January 2001), p. 21.

47. For example, one of the co-conspirators in the 1993 World Trade Center attack and two members of the Real IRA, a terrorist group that had broken away from the Irish Republican Army. See Testimony of Glenn Fine, Inspector General, U.S. Department of Justice, *Technology's Role in Preventing the Entry of Terrorists*

into the United States, Hearing before the Senate Judiciary Subcommittee on Technology, Terrorism, and Government Information, 107 Cong. 1 sess. (October 12, 2001), p. 3.

48. A 1999 sample of 1,067 stolen passports in VWP countries found that over half the stolen documents had no lookout record and almost 10 percent may have been successfully used to gain entry into the United States. Also, in 1999, INS inspectors had an average of less than one minute to process VWP visitors and sometimes did not check the lookout system. Fine, Hearing, pp. 3–4.

49. Testimony of Peter M. Becraft, INS Deputy Commissioner, *Visa Waiver Program,* Hearing before the House Judiciary Subcommittee on Immigration and Claims, 107 Cong. 2 sess. (February 28, 2002).

50. Testimony of James Ziglar, INS Commissioner (October 17, 2001).

51. Peter T. Kilborn, "Your Thumb Here: Newest ID of Choice at Store and on Job," *New York Times,* February 20, 2002, p. 1.

52. Edward Bannerman and others, *Europe after September 11* (London: Centre for European Reform, 2001), p. 9.

53. Flynn, "Beyond Border Control," p. 57.

54. Fine, Hearing, p. 4.

55. Ryan, Hearing.

56. A 1998 study by the Inspector General, U.S. Justice Department, found that information for less than two-thirds of apprehended aliens was recorded in the IDENT database. Also, the study concluded that "INS program offices, such as Investigations and Intelligence, viewed IDENT as a Border Patrol initiative." See Fine, Hearing, p. 7.

Chapter 3

1. Statement of Francis Gallagher, Deputy Assistant Director, Criminal Division, Organized Crime, Drugs, Violent Crimes and Major Offenders Branch, Federal Bureau of Investigation, Hearing before the House Committee on Government Reform, 107 Cong. 1 sess. (December 5, 2001).

2. President George W. Bush, *Securing the Homeland, Strengthening the Nation* (February 2002), www.whitehouse.gov/homeland/homeland_security_book.pdf.

3. Gallagher, Hearing before the House Committee on Government Reform.

4. General Accounting Office, *Foreign Languages: Human Capital Approach Needed to Correct Staffing and Proficiency Shortfalls,* GAO-02-375 (January 2002).

5. Ham and Atkinson, "Using Technology to Detect and Prevent Terrorism."

6. Testimony of Glenn Fine, Inspector General, U.S. Department of Justice, *Technology's Role in Preventing the Entry of Terrorists into the United States,* Hearing before the Senate Judiciary Subcommittee on Technology, Terrorism, and Government Information, 107 Cong. 1 sess. (October 12, 2001), p. 4.

7. Ibid., p. 6.

8. General Accounting Office, *Information Technology: INS Needs to Better Manage the Development of Its Enterprise Architecture*, GAO/AIMD-00-212 (August 2000), and *Information Technology: INS Needs to Strengthen Its Investment in Management Capability*, GAO-01-146 (December 2000).

9. Statement of Kathleen McChesney, Assistant Director, Training Division, Federal Bureau of Investigation, Hearing before the Committee on Government Reform, U.S. House of Representatives, 107 Cong. 1 sess. (November 13, 2001).

10. Shane Ham and Robert D. Atkinson, "Using Technology to Detect and Prevent Terrorism," Progressive Policy Institute (January 2002).

11. Statement of Tim Hoescht, Senior Vice President for Technology, Oracle Service Industries, Hearing before the Committee on Government Reform, Subcommittee on Government Efficiency, Financial Management, and Intergovernmental Relations, U.S. House of Representatives, 107 Cong. 1 sess. (November 16, 2001).

12. Robert O'Harrow Jr., "States Seek National ID Funds: Motor Vehicle Group Backs High-Tech Driver's Licenses," *Washington Post*, January 14, 2002, p. A4.

13. American Association of Motor Vehicle Administrators, "AAMVA Helps Secure a Safer America, Recommends Driver's License/ID Security Improvements" (January 14, 2002).

14. Century Foundation, "National ID Card FAQ," available at www.tcf.org.

15. William Welsh, "Think a National ID System Is Too Costly? Think Again," *Washington Technology* (December 14, 2001), available at www.washtech.com. The *Washington Post*, however, reports that the same association has estimated the costs to be between $70 million and $100 million. See O'Harrow, "States Seek National ID Funds: Motor Vehicle Group Backs High-Tech Driver's Licenses."

16. Alex Salkever and John Cady, "The Price of Protecting the Airways: From Slick Data Sifters to Biometric Analysis, Businesses Have Lots of New Proposals for Making Airports Safer, but Who'll Foot the Bills?" *Business Week Online*, December 10, 2001.

17. Barry Steinhardt, Associate Director of the American Civil Liberties Union, Address to the American Association of Motor Vehicle Administrators, February 10, 2002.

18. Ham and Atkinson, "Using Technology to Detect and Prevent Terrorism."

19. In 1997, 64 percent of the value and 56 percent of the weight of hazardous materials shipments were transported by truck. See *Statistical Abstract of the United States 2000*, table 1013, p. 621.

20. Battelle, "Comparative Risks of Hazardous Materials and Non-Hazardous Materials Truck Shipment Accidents/Incidents," prepared for the Federal Motor Carrier Safety Administration (March 2001).

21. See *Bus and Truck Security and Hazardous Materials Licensing*, Hearing before the Senate Subcommittee on Surface Transportation and Merchant Marine, Senate

Committee on Commerce, Science, and Transportation, 107 Cong. 1 sess. (October 10, 2001), pp. 3, 6, 25, 36, 37; and Evelyn Nieves with Andrew C. Revkin, "Urgent Efforts to Bar Use of Stolen Trucks as Bombs," *New York Times*, November 18, 2001, p. B8.

22. Fredrick Kunkle, "States Put Their Own Spins on Inspecting 18-Wheelers," *Washington Post*, November 25, 2001, p. C1.

23. James C. Belke, "Chemical Accident Risks in U.S. Industry" (Washington: U.S. Environmental Protection Agency, September 25, 2000).

24. Raymond McCaffrey, "Risk of Gas Tankers in Bay Revisited," *Washington Post*, December 5, 2001, p. B3.

25. See www.oit.doe.gov/chemicals/profile.shtml.

26. Belke, "Chemical Accident Risks in U.S. industry."

27. Ibid.

28. Eric Pianin, "Study Assesses Risk of Attack on Chemical Plant," *Washington Post*, March 12, 2002, p. A8. See also Jeremiah Baumann, "Protecting Our Hometowns: Preventing Chemical Terrorism in America," U.S. Public Interest Research Group Education Fund, March 7, 2002.

29. Rick Hind, "Is the U.S. Chemical Industry Our Weakest Link against Terrorist Attacks?" available at www.greenpeaceusa.org.

30. Eric Pianin, "Toxic Chemicals' Security Worries Officials," *Washington Post*, November 12, 2001, p. A14.

31. Ibid. For an upper bound on the costs of tightened security at such a site, the on-site monitoring arrangements under certain arms control treaties can be a useful model; see Congressional Budget Office, *U.S. Costs of Verification and Compliance under Pending Arms Treaties* (Washington, 1990), pp. 18–19.

32. Congressional Budget Office, Cost Estimate on H.R. 3016, October 17, 2001; and *Wall Street Journal*, "Corrections and Amplifications," October 17, 2001.

33. Joby Warrick and Steve Fainarum, "Access to Microbes Is Easily Obtained," *WashTech*, October 28, 2001, available at www.washtech.com.

34. *Statistical Abstract of the United States* 2000, table 962.

35. See, for example, Richard L. Garwin and Georges Charpak, *Megawatts and Megatons* (Alfred A. Knopf, 2001), p. 202.

36. Letter from David Lochbaum, Union of Concerned Scientists, to Office of Nuclear Reactor Regulation, Nuclear Regulatory Commission, "Protection against Radiological Sabotage by Insider(s)," November 29, 2001.

37. Letter from Richard Meserve, chair, NRC, to Rep. Edward Markey, March 4, 2002.

38. Lochbaum, Letter.

39. Union of Concerned Scientists, "Briefing on Nuclear Reactor Security," available at www.ucsusa.org/energy/br_saferplants.html.

40. Ibid.; and Michael Grunwald and Peter Behr, "Are Nation's Nuclear Power Plants Secure?" *Washington Post*, November 4, 2001, p. A16.

41. "Obey the Rules," *Economist*, December 22, 2001.

42. Grunwald and Behr, "Are Nation's Nuclear Power Plants Secure?"

43. In some states, such as New Jersey, guards at nuclear facilities are not allowed to use a wide range of weapons. Richard Meserve, Chairman, Nuclear Regulatory Commission, November 1, 2001.

Chapter 4

1. The very fact of their size means that large office or residential structures pose a greater concern compared with smaller or more dispersed structures. In chapter 6 we discuss the utility of insurance and other mechanisms as a way to change the incentives around structure size and design.

2. See S. Fred Singer, "Nuclear Terrorism: Facts and Fantasies," *Washington Times*, April 5, 2002, p. 19; John Meyer, "Nuclear Plants Said to Face Big Attack Risk," *Los Angeles Times*, March 26, 2002, p. 1.

3. See U.S. Army Corps of Engineers, "Protecting Buildings and Their Occupants from Airborne Hazards," draft, October 2001.

4. Energy Information Administration, Department of Energy, "Building Characteristics: Buildings Use Tables," table 12, available at www.eia.doe.gov/emeu/consumption.

5. Ibid.

6. Letter from Michael C. Janus, Battelle Corporation, December 1, 2001, to Michael O'Hanlon.

7. Ann Gerhart, "Tom Ridge, on High Alert," *Washington Post*, November 12, 2001, p. C1.

8. Statement of Arden Bement, Director, National Institute of Standards and Technology, Hearing before the Committee on Science, U.S. House of Representatives, 107 Cong. 2 sess. (March 6, 2002). See also Eric Lipton and James Glanz, "New Rules Proposed to Help High-Rises Withstand Attacks," *New York Times*, March 6, 2002, p. A1.

9. For measures that could be adopted for smaller buildings if necessary, see Yaakov Yerushalmi, Uzi More, and Amit Reizes, "Design Techniques to Strengthen 'Soft Buildings' against Acts of Terror and Car Bombs" (Gaithersburg, Md.: Scientech Inc., March 2002).

10. See http://beta.collectingchannel.com/?page=welcome/stadiums.

11. Neely Tucker and Petula Dvorak, "Lapses Plague Security at Federal Buildings," *Washington Post*, September 28, 2001.

12. "Mixed Security Found at Federal Buildings in Washington," *Government Executive*, October 18, 2001.

13. Bernard Ungar, *General Services Administration: Status of Efforts to Improve Management of Building Security Upgrade Program*, GAO/T-GGD/OSI-00-19 (General Accounting Office, October 7, 1999).

14. A study commissioned by the National Park Service had documented significant security gaps at prominent monuments, although the study's methodology has been sharply criticized. See Arthur Santana, "Monuments Are Found Vulnerable to Attack," *Washington Post*, July 2, 2000; and Statement of John Parachini, Center for Nonproliferation Studies, Monterey Institute of International Studies, Hearing before the Committee on Government Reform, Subcommittee on National Security, Veterans Affairs, and International Relations, U.S. House of Representatives, 106 Cong. 2 sess. (July 26, 2000).

15. Heritage Foundation Homeland Security Task Force, *Defending the American Homeland* (Washington: Heritage Foundation, 2002), p. 15.

16. President's Commission on Critical Infrastructure Protection, *Critical Foundations: Protecting America's Infrastructures* (October 1997), p. A-27.

17. "Utilities Can Raise Rates to Pay for Security," Bloomberg Report, September 14, 2001.

18. President's Commission, *Critical Foundations*, p. 12.

19. Ibid., p. A-45.

20. Yochi J. Dreazen, "Officials Fear Terrorists Could Use 'Backflow' to Push Toxins into Water-Distribution Grids," *Wall Street Journal*, December 27, 2001.

21. Josh Meyer and Aaron Zitner, "Troops Uncovered Diagrams for Major U.S. Targets, Bush Says," *Los Angeles Times*, January 30, 2002, p. 1. On the difficulty of contaminating large amounts of water with chemical or biological agents, see President's Commission, *Critical Foundations*, pp. A-45–A46.

22. Tony Pugh, "$3 Billion Sought to Sanitize Mail," *Miami Herald*, December 25, 2001.

23. Robert Robinson, *Food Safety and Security: Fundamental Changes Needed to Ensure Safe Food*, GAO-02-47T (General Accounting Office, October 10, 2001).

24. "Scrutiny Gap Seen in Imported Foods," *San Antonio Express-News*, November 16, 2001.

25. Tommy G. Thompson, "Food Safety and America's Future," remarks before the National Food Processors Association, Washington, D.C., November 27, 2001.

26. Current USDA foreign inspection efforts leave much to be desired. See Joby Warrick, "USDA Relies on Foreign Inspections: Meat Plants Abroad Fail Sanitation Checks," *Washington Post*, Monday, February 25, 2002, p. A01.

27. For further discussion, see John C. Bailar III, "Ensuring Safe Food: An Organizational Perspective," in Scott P. Layne, Tony J. Beugelsdijk, and C. Kumar N. Patel, eds., *Firepower in the Lab: Automation in the Fight against Infectious Diseases and Bioterrorism* (National Academy of Sciences: Washington, 2000); and Institute of Medicine and National Research Council, *Ensuring Safe Food: From Production to Consumption* (National Academy of Sciences: Washington, 1998).

28. Robinson, "Food Safety and Security." Several earlier GAO reports also called for the same reforms.

29. Arnaud Borchgrave and others. "Cyber Threats and Information Security

Meeting the 21st Century Challenge" (Washington: Center for Strategic and International Studies, December 2000).

30. The General Accounting Office has documented numerous security flaws in government computer systems. See, for example, General Accounting Office, *Information Security: Serious and Widespread Weaknesses Persist at Federal Agencies,* GAO/AIMD-00-295 (September 2000).

31. Renae Merle, "IT [Information Technology] Group Says Security Is Underfunded," *Washington Post,* February 1, 2002, p. E5.

32. The Office of Personnel Management has proposed a new "Senior Civil Service," comprising two corps: the Senior Executive Corps (SEC) and the Senior Professional Corps (SPC). The purpose of the reform would be to provide the same level of prestige and attractiveness to the two corps, thus eliminating the current discrepancy between the Senior Executive Service and SL/ST positions; under the new plan, senior government officials who were truly fulfilling executive functions would enter the SEC, whereas senior technical experts would enter the SPC. Increasing the attractiveness of the civil service for technical workers—as this reform would—could help to induce highly skilled computer programmers to join the government.

33. See, for example, Michelle Delio, "GovNet: What Is It Good For?" *Wired News,* January 21, 2002.

34. National Research Council, *Cybersecurity Today and Tomorrow: Pay Now or Pay Later* (Washington: National Academy of Sciences Press, 2002), p. 9.

35. "A Battle-Ready Net?" *Business Week,* October 1, 2001.

36. Heritage Foundation Homeland Security Task Force, *Defending the American Homeland,* p. 19.

37. The Aviation Security Act funds research and development for technologies that will enhance airline security. Of the $70 million authorized for annual appropriations, $20 million is for research on biometrics, long-term airport security, and security information sharing among federal agencies. The act also authorizes R&D on detection of chemical and biological weapons on airplanes. According to the CBO, outlays for this R&D would total $73 million over 2002–06.

38. Stephanie Stoughton, "At Top Speed Facing Deadlines, Airports Push U.S. for Decisions, Funds," *Boston Globe,* January 26, 2002.

39. The aviation security law required all checked luggage to be screened by January 18, 2002. But the requisite machines will not be ready, and the alternatives to machine-screening provided by the law (such as matching bags to boarded passengers, manual search, canine search, or other methods approved by the under secretary of transportation for security) will impose significant costs on airlines and travelers, and potentially be less effective.

40. Testimony of Mark Dayton, Deputy Assistant Inspector General, U.S. Department of Transportation, Hearing before the Senate Committee on Commerce, Science, and Transportation, 107 Cong. 1 sess. (November 1, 2001).

41. See Brian Michael Jenkins and Larry N. Gersten, "Protecting Public Surface Transportation against Terrorism and Serious Crime: Continuing Research on Best Security Practices" (San Jose, Calif.: Mineta Transportation Institute, San Jose State University, 2001).

42. Lyndsey Layton, "Metro Set to Initiate Chemical Sensors; Use at 2 D.C. Stations a First for Subways," *Washington Post*, December 25, 2001, p. A01.

43. Lyndsey Layton, "Metro Seeks High-Tech Security," *Washington Post*, October 16, 2001, p. B1.

44. The Rail Security Act, introduced in the Senate, combines appropriations for operating security expenses, tunnel upgrades, other short-term capital projects, and increasing the accessibility of Penn Station for safety reasons. The cost for improvements at Penn Station alone is $254 million, and the CBO estimates the entire bill would cost $1.3 billion over 2002–06, and an additional $450 million afterward. The Bush administration has expressed opposition to the capital spending and long-term expenses in the bill, which has not yet received a vote before the full Senate.

Chapter 5

1. Most biological weapons detectors in use today require wet samples; they cannot provide continuous monitoring of the surrounding air. See David Talbot, "Detecting Bioterrorism," *Technology Review* (December 2001), p. 35; Kenneth Chang and Andrew Pollack, "Developing an Early Warning System for a Biological Attack Proves Difficult," *New York Times*, October 28, 2001, p. B2.

2. Costs estimated from costs of current R&D programs at weapons laboratories on chemical and biological detectors.

3. For useful findings on this subject, developed before September 11, see CSIS Homeland Defense Project, *Combating Chemical, Biological, Radiological, and Nuclear Terrorism: A Comprehensive Strategy* (Washington: Center for Strategic and International Studies, 2001).

4. Amy Smithson and Leslie-Anne Levy, *Ataxia: The Chemical and Biological Terrorism Threat and the US Response*, Henry L. Stimson Center Report 35 (October 2000), p. 292.

5. Advisory Panel to Assess Domestic Response Capabilities for Terrorism Involving Weapons of Mass Destruction (the Gilmore Panel), *Toward a National Strategy for Combating Terrorism*, second annual report (Arlington, Va.: December 2000), pp. G-15–G-16; Smithson and Levy, *Ataxia*, p. xiv.

6. Joint Commission on Accreditation of Healthcare Organizations (hereafter JCAHO), *Joint Commission Perspectives*, Special Issue (December 2001), p. 5.

7. Smithson and Levy, *Ataxia*, p. 310.

8. For other perspectives on required increases, see Richard Falkenrath, Robert Newman, and Bradley Thayer, *America's Achilles' Heel* (MIT Press, 1998), p. 302; As

a rough estimate for one category of expenses, it could cost up to $1,000 per person for a gas mask, gloves, protective clothing, and related equipment. Scaling by population with a proposal for Washington, D.C., and thus assuming enough equipment for about 250,000 public employees, would translate into $250 million in total cost. See Lyndsey Layton, "Metro Seeks High-Tech Security," *Washington Post*, October 16, 2001, p. B1.

9. Arnold F. Kaufmann, Martin I. Meltzer, and George P. Schmid, "The Economic Impact of a Bioterrorist Attack: Are Prevention and Postattack Intervention Programs Justifiable?" *Emerging Infectious Diseases*, vol. 3, no. 2; Donald Clark Wetter, William Edward Daniell, and Charles David Treser, "Hospital Preparedness for Victims of Chemical or Biological Terrorism," *American Journal of Public Health*, vol. 91 (May 2001), pp. 710–16.

10. JCAHO, *Joint Commission Perspectives*, pp. 2–3; Janet Heinrich, *Bioterrorism: Public Health and Medical Preparedness*, GAO-02-141T (General Accounting Office, October 9, 2001), p. 14.

11. John G. Bartlett, "Applying Lessons Learned from Anthrax Case History to Other Scenarios," *Emerging Infectious Diseases*, vol. 5 (July–August 1999), pp. 561–63.

12. American Hospital Association, "Hospital Resources for Disaster Readiness," available at www.aha.org

13. JCAHO, *Joint Commission Perspectives*, p. 3.

14. Ibid., p. 13.

15. Ibid., p. 3.

16. Donald Clark Wetter, William Edward Daniell, and Charles David Treser, "Hospital Preparedness for Victims of Chemical or Biological Terrorism," *American Journal of Public Health*, vol. 91 (May 2001), p. 714.

17. Smithson and Levy, *Ataxia*, p. xv.

18. JCAHO, *Joint Commission Perspectives*, p. 20.

19. American Hospital Association, "Hospital Resources for Disaster Readiness."

20. Smithson and Levy, *Ataxia*, p. 311.

21. American Hospital Association, "Hospital Resources for Disaster Readiness."

22. JCAHO, *Joint Commission Perspectives*, pp. 10, 13.

23. Monica Schoch-Spana, "Hospitals Buckle during Normal Flu Season: Implications for Bioterrorism Response," *Biodefense Quarterly*, vol. 1, no. 4 (2000), Center for Civilian Biodefense Studies, Johns Hopkins University (www.hopkins-biodefense.org/pages/news/quarter1_4.html), downloaded January 8, 2002, pp. 1, 4.

24. Smithson and Levy, *Ataxia*, p. xv.

25. National Press Club Luncheon with Anthony Principi, Secretary, U.S. Department of Veterans' Affairs, November 6, 2001. Transcript downloaded from LexisNexis January 3, 2002, p. 5.

26. American Hospital Association, "Hospital Resources for Disaster Readiness."

27. Cynthia Bascetta, "Homeland Security: Need to Consider VA's Role in

Strengthening Federal Preparedness," GAO-02-145T (General Accounting Office, October 15, 2001), p. 5.

28. Smithson and Levy, *Ataxia*, p. xxi; American Hospital Association, "Hospital Resources for Disaster Readiness."

29. JCAHO, *Joint Commission Perspectives*, p. 18.

30. Jacob H. Fries, "Spy Store Sales Are Now Driven by 9/11, Not 007," *New York Times*, February 20, 2002, p. A20.

31. President George W. Bush, *Securing the Homeland, Strengthening the Nation* (February 2002), p. 21.

32. American Hospital Association, "Hospital Resources for Disaster Readiness."

33. Ceci Connolly, "Bioterrorism Defense Plan Called Inadequate," *Washington Post*, October 23, 2000, p. A11.

34. American Hospital Association, "Hospital Resources for Disaster Readiness."

35. Ibid.

36. JCAHO, *Joint Commission Perspectives*, p. 10.

37. American Hospital Association, "Hospital Resources for Disaster Readiness."

38. Ibid.

39. See, for example, John A. T. Young and R. John Collier, "Attacking Anthrax," *Scientific American* (March 2002), pp. 48–59.

40. Justin Gillis, "Scientists Race for Vaccines," *Washington Post*, November 8, 2001, p. E1.

41. Heinrich, *Bioterrorism*, pp. 4–5.

Chapter 6

1. Even in such areas, the private sector has a substantial and crucial role to play, although the government remains the natural leader.

2. Statement of Bob Bostock, assistant EPA administrator for homeland security, quoted in James Grimaldi and Guy Gugliotta, "Chemical Plants Are Feared as Targets," *Washington Post*, December 16, 2001, p. A1.

3. Supporters of a voluntary approach to security measures may argue that the only required form of government intervention is the legal liability system, through which courts require actors held responsible for damages to others to provide compensation. In theory, the threat of liability does provide incentives to private actors to take precautions to minimize exposures to—and damages from—terrorism that affects third parties and thus could address the negative externality from terrorism. In practice, however, the liability system by itself is unlikely to generate a reasonably efficient response by the private sector to the terrorist threat. Appendix A examines the legal liability system in more detail.

4. For further discussion of "contamination" effects, see Howard Kunreuther and Geoffrey Heal, "Interdependent Security: The Case of Identical Agents" (Cambridge, Mass.: National Bureau of Economic Research, February 2002).

5. It is also possible, at least in theory, for private firms to invest *too much* in antiterrorism security. In particular, visible security measures (such as more uniformed guards) undertaken by one firm may merely displace terrorist attacks onto other firms, without significantly affecting the overall probability of an attack. In such a scenario, the total security precautions undertaken can escalate beyond the socially desirable levels, and government intervention could theoretically improve matters by placing *limits* on how much security firms would undertake. Unobservable security precautions (which are difficult for potential terrorists to detect), on the other hand, do not displace vulnerabilities from one firm to another and can at least theoretically reduce the overall level of terrorism activity. For an interesting application of these ideas to the Lojack automobile security system, see Ian Ayres and Steven Levitt, "Measuring Positive Externalities from Unobservable Victim Precaution: An Empirical Analysis of Lojack," *Quarterly Journal of Economics,* vol. 113, no. 1 (February 1998), pp. 43–77. See also Peter Orszag and Joseph Stiglitz, "Optimal Fire Departments: Evaluating Public Policy in the Face of Externalities," Working Paper (Brookings, January 2002).

6. The Coase theorem shows that under very restrictive conditions, the negative externality can be corrected by voluntary private actions even if the role of government is limited to enforcing property rights. But the Coase theorem requires that all affected parties be able to negotiate at sufficiently low cost with each other. Since virtually the entire nation could be affected indirectly by a terrorist attack, the costs of negotiation are prohibitive, making the Coase theorem essentially irrelevant in the terrorism context.

7. For further discussion of this issue in the context of natural disasters, see David Moss, *When All Else Fails* (Harvard University Press, 2002).

8. As the great British economist Alfred Marshall emphasized, "A Government could print a good edition of Shakespeare's works, but it could not get them written. . . . Every new extension of Governmental work in branches of production which need ceaseless creation and initiative is to be regarded as prima facie antisocial, because it retards the growth of that knowledge and those ideas which are incomparably the most important form of collective wealth." Alfred Marshall, "The Social Possibilities of Economic Chivalry," *Economic Journal,* vol. 17 (March 1907), pp. 7–29.

9. Although building codes traditionally fall within the jurisdiction of local governments, the Americans with Disabilities Act (ADA) mandated changes in buildings. A precedent therefore exists for federal preemption of local building codes. It should be noted that the ADA does not directly affect existing building codes. But the legislation requires changes in building access and permits the attorney general to certify that a state law, local building code, or similar ordinance "meets or exceeds the minimum accessibility requirements" for public accommodations and commercial facilities under the ADA. Such certification is considered "rebuttable evidence" that the state law or local ordinance meets or exceeds the minimum requirements of the ADA.

10. The McCarren-Ferguson Act delegates insurance regulation to the states. The federal government could nonetheless effectively impose an insurance mandate either by providing strong incentives to the states to adopt such a mandate, or perhaps by mandating that all commercial loans from a federally related financial institution require the borrower to hold such insurance.

11. In theory, the different approaches to implementing a security measure could be separated from how the costs of the measure were financed. For example, firms adhering to regulatory standards could be reimbursed by the federal budget for their costs. In practice, however, the method of implementation often implies a method of financing: the cost of regulations will be borne by the producers and users of a service, and the cost of a general subsidy will be borne by taxpayers as a whole. In evaluating different implementation strategies, financing implications must therefore be taken into account.

12. A further complication in this context, as in any other given regulatory setting, is how to value the damage avoided: specifically, whether to apply monetary values to lives saved and injuries avoided, and if so, how. We take as a given that, in principle, such valuations can be done, as they are in other regulatory contexts, but we also note that they remain controversial. For a guide to the issues involved in placing monetary values on human lives and injuries saved or avoided, see, for example, Kenneth Arrow and others, *Benefit-Cost Analysis in Environmental, Health, and Safety Regulation: A Statement of Principle,* (Washington: American Enterprise Institute, 1996).

13. Fines could be adopted as part of the regulatory system to ensure compliance with minimum standards for preventative measures.

14. In other words, an antiterrorism standard for, say, athletic arenas could impose an excessively tight standard (which would involve unnecessary costs) or an excessively loose standard (which would involve insufficient protection against terrorist threats).

15. For example, in the environmental context, placing the same limit on emissions of harmful substances by all firms or individuals ignores the differences in costs of preventing pollution. That is why economists have long advocated market-based approaches to emission reductions, such as a permit trading system (which is currently in place for sulfur dioxide emissions) or a tax on emissions. Either market-based approach to regulation can achieve the same level of environmental protection at lower overall cost than a regulatory approach because it encourages those who can most cheaply control pollution to do so (to avoid paying for the permit or the tax). A key requirement for a permit trading system or a tax, however, is some method of measuring "outcomes," such as the monitoring of pollution emitted by parties subject to the tax or participating in the system. In the context of antiterrorism measures, the appropriate metric would be related to the expected loss from a terrorist attack. Yet it is difficult to see how such expected losses could be quantified and thus provide the basis for a permit trading system or a tax.

16. For more extensive discussion of innovative regulatory approaches, see Cary Coglianese and David Lazer, "Management-Based Regulatory Approaches," in John D. Donahue and Joseph S. Nye Jr., eds., *Market-Based Governance* (Brookings, 2002).

17. *Blue Chip Economic Indicators,* vol. 26, no. 9 (September 10, 2001).

18. The insurance requirement would complement the use of the liability system to encourage protective measures: insurance coverage would be relatively more important in the context of large liability exposures.

19. By similar reasoning, insurers should not be able to use genetic information to discriminate in rates charged for health coverage since individuals cannot control their genetic makeup.

20. As discussed in the text below, universal insurance could arise without a government mandate if it is required by private-sector lenders.

21. See Howard Kunreuther, "Risk Management and Extreme Events: The Role of Insurance and Protective Measures," paper presented at the First Paris International Conference on Risk and Insurance Economics, Paris, December 11, 2001. For further analysis of the Pool Re and other programs abroad, see General Accounting Office, *Terrorism Insurance: Alternative Programs for Protecting Insurance Consumers* GAO-02-199T (October 24, 2001); and Congressional Budget Office (CBO), *Federal Reinsurance for Terrorism Risks* (October 2001).

22. CBO, *Federal Reinsurance for Terrorism Risks.*

23. J. Robert Hunter, "How the Lack of Federal Back Up for Terrorism Insurance Affected Insurers and Consumers: An Analysis of Market Conditions and Policy Implications," Consumer Federation of America, January 23, 2002.

24. Michele Heller, "No Terror Insurance, but Lenders Still Lending," *The American Banker,* January 7, 2002.

25. For further discussion of the issues involved in federal reinsurance, see CBO, *Federal Reinsurance for Terrorism Risks.*

26. Testimony of Kenneth Froot, Hearing before the U.S. Senate Committee on Banking, Housing, and Urban Affairs, 107 Cong. 1 sess. (October 24, 2001).

27. One argument against a government backstop insurance mechanism is that it could forestall the development of privately offered "terrorism bonds," or securities that would spread the risk of terrorist incidents across many investors (by having cancellation of interest, and possibly principal, in the event of a terrorist attack). In the wake of September 11, however, it is unlikely that such a market would develop: investors would demand too much of an interest premium over safe securities (such as government bonds) for private insurers (the most likely issuers of such securities) to offer them. For similar reasons, the market in "catastrophe bonds"—which cover hurricane and earthquake risks—has been very slow to develop. For further discussion of catastrophe bonds, see Vivek Bantwal and Howard Kunreuther, "A Cat Bond Premium Puzzle?" Financial Institutions Center, Wharton School, University of Pennsylvania, May 1999; and Kenneth Froot, ed., *The Financing of Catastrophic Risk* (University of Chicago Press, 1999).

28. See, for example, Testimony of David Moss, Hearing before the U.S. Senate Committee on Commerce, Science, and Transportation, 107 Cong. 1 sess. (October 30, 2001).

29. For alternatives to a federal reinsurance program, see Hunter, "How the Lack of Federal Back Up for Terrorism Insurance Affected Insurers and Consumers."

30. See, for example, Kenneth Froot, "The Market for Catastrophic Risk: A Clinical Examination," Working Paper 8110 (Cambridge, Mass.: National Bureau of Economic Research, February 2001).

31. In principle, the government could also tax firms that failed to implement security measures. This approach does not appear to be remotely politically viable and is, therefore, not discussed here.

32. Consider, for example, a tax credit equal to 50 percent of the cost of building improvements that protect against terrorism. Such a high subsidy rate may encourage firms to undertake too much investment in security against terrorism, in the sense that the costs of the investment are not fully justified by the protections they provide against terrorism. For example, reinforced windows may provide protection against shattering in the event of a terrorist attack. Even if the protection provided is minimal, the firm may find it worthwhile to undertake the investment since so much of the cost is borne by others, and since the reinforced windows may provide other benefits (such as reduced heating and cooling costs because of the added insulation). Relatedly, a subsidy provides a strong incentive for firms to classify changes that would have otherwise been undertaken as "antiterrorism" measures in order to qualify for the subsidy.

33. Lobbying would undoubtedly occur in the context of a regulatory approach, but since regulations are made on the basis of some kind of evidentiary record and are subject to judicial review, the room for lobbying is restricted. In contrast, subsidies are expenditures of the government and are handed out by Congress, which is inherently much more amenable to lobbying.

34. Alan Auerbach, William Gale, and Peter Orszag, "The Budget Outlook and Options for Fiscal Policy" (Brookings, April 2002).

35. See, for example, Moody's Investors Service, "Moody's Approach to Terrorism Insurance for U.S. Commercial Real Estate," March 1, 2002. See also Christopher Oster, "Can the Risk of Terrorism Be Calculated by Insurers? Game Theory Might Do It," Wall Street Journal, April 8, 2002.

36. Moreover, an insurance *requirement* (as opposed to an insurance option) avoids the adverse selection problem that can occur in voluntary insurance settings. In particular, if antiterrorism insurance were not mandatory, firms with the most severe terrorism exposure would be the most likely to demand insurance against terrorist acts. The insurance companies, which may have less information about the exposure to terrorism than the firms themselves, may therefore be hesitant to offer insurance against terrorist attacks, since the worst risks would disproportionately want such insurance. The outcome could be either that the insurance companies do

not offer the insurance, or that they charge such a high price for it that many firms (with lower exposure to terrorism but nonetheless some need to purchase insurance against it) find it unattractive. In the face of constraints or imperfections on the supply side of the insurance market, the relative costs and benefits of mandatory versus voluntary insurance may change.

37. For a discussion of the potential benefits of a mixed system of building code regulations and mandatory catastrophic risk insurance in the context of natural disasters, see Peter Diamond, "Comment on Catastrophic Risk Management," in Froot, *The Financing of Catastrophic Risk,* pp. 85–88, and Paul R. Kleindorfer and Howard Kunreuther, "The Complementary Roles of Mitigation and Insurance in Managing Catastrophic Risks," *Risk Analysis,* vol. 19, no. 4 (1999), pp. 727–38.

38. See, for example, Wallace Oates, *Fiscal Federalism* (Harcourt Brace Jovanovich, 1972).

Chapter 7

1. This chapter draws heavily on the following works by Ivo Daalder and I. M. Destler: Statement Prepared for Hearings before the U.S. Senate Committee on Governmental Affairs, October 12, 2001, and April 11, 2002; "Enhancing Homeland Security: Organizational Options," paper prepared for the Century Foundation's Task Force on U.S. Homeland Security, February 2002; and "Organizing for Homeland Security," *National Interest,* no. 68 (Summer 2002), forthcoming.

2. Dwight D. Eisenhower, *The White House Years: Mandate for Change, 1953–1956* (Doubleday, 1963), p. 114.

3. Office of Management and Budget, *Annual Report to Congress on Combating Terrorism* (August 2001), available at www.whitehouse.gov/omb/legislative/ nsd_annual_report2001.pdf (October 2001).

4. See Alison Mitchell, "Disputes Erupt on Ridge's Needs for His Job," *New York Times,* November 4, 2001, p. B7.

5. *Road Map for National Security: Imperative for Change,* Phase III Report of the U.S. Commission on National Security/21st Century, March 15, 2001, co-chaired by Gary Hart and Warren B. Rudman.

6. See *National Homeland Security Agency Act,* H. Rept. 1158, 107 Cong. 1 sess. (GPO, 2001), introduced by Representative Mac Thornberry, March 21, 2001; and *Department of National Homeland Security Act of 2001,* S. Rept. 1534, 107 Cong. 1 sess. (GPO, 2001), introduced by Senators Joe Lieberman and Arlen Specter, October 11, 2001.

7. *Third Annual Report to the President and the Congress: II,* for Ray Downey, December 15, 2001, chaired by Governor James S. Gilmore III, p. 3.

8. Prepared Statement of Gen. Barry McCaffrey (Ret.), Hearing before the Senate Governmental Affairs Committee, October 12, 2001, available at www.senate.gov/~gov_affairs/101201mccaffrey.htm (February 2002).

9. Executive Order Establishing Office of Homeland Security, October 8, 2001, Sec. 5(a), available at www.whitehouse.gov/news/releases/2001/10/20011008-2.html (January 2002).

10. Homeland Security Presidential Directive-1, October 29, 2001, available at www.whitehouse.gov/ news/releases/2001/10/print/20011030-1.html (accessed November 2001); and National Security Presidential Directive-1, February 13, 2001, available at www.fas.org/irp/offdocs/nspd/nspd-1.htm (January 2002).

11. Alison Mitchell, "Ridge Is Opening a Center to Analyze and Share Data," *New York Times*, December 25, 2001, p. B5.

12. Hart quoted in David Corn, "Ridge on the Ledge," *Nation*, November 18, 2001.

13. I. M. Destler, *The National Economic Council: A Work in Progress*, Policy Analysis 46 (Institute for International Economics, November 1996), p. 14; Bob Woodward, *The Agenda: Inside the Clinton White House* (New York: Pocket Books, 1995), chap. 11.

14. Executive Order Establishing the Office of Homeland Security, Sec. 3(a).

15. President George W. Bush, *Securing the Homeland, Strengthening the Nation* (Washington, January 2002), p. 7. Available at www.whitehouse.gov/homeland/homeland_security_book.html (February 2002).

16. Ashton B. Carter, "The Architecture of Government in the Face of Terrorism," *International Security*, vol. 26 (Winter 2001/2002), p. 13.

17. Executive Order Establishing the Office of Homeland Security, Sec. 3(I).

18. Steve Brill, "Ridge against the Machine," *Newsweek*, March 18, 2002, p. 34.

19. Joel Brinkley and Philip Shenon, "Ridge Meeting Opposition from Agencies," *New York Times*, February 7, 2002, p. A12.

20. Brill, "Ridge against the Machine," p. 34.

21. Executive Order Establishing the Office of Homeland Security, Sec. 3(g).

22. Alison Mitchell, "First Test for a Disaster Response Plan," *New York Times*, November 13, 2001, p. A19.

23. Mitchell, "Ridge Is Opening a Center," p. B5.

24. See Anthony Lake, *Six Nightmares* (Little, Brown, 2000), p. 60.

25. Quoted in Tim Weiner, "U.S. and Mexico to Share Work at the Border," *New York Times*, March 6, 2002, p. A8.

26. Alison Mitchell, "Official Urges Combining Several Agencies to Create One That Protects Borders," *New York Times*, January 12, 2002, p. A8.

27. "Border Security White Paper," The White House, December 21, 2001, pp. 1–2.

28. Eric Pianin and Bill Miller, "For Ridge, Ambitions and Reality Clash," *Washington Post*, January 23, 2002, p. A1.

29. "Statement of the President and Governor Ridge," The White House, Office of the Press Secretary, October 8, 2001, available at www.whitehouse.gov/news/releases/2001/10/20011008-3.html (March 2002).

30. David Sanger and Eric Schmitt, "Bush Leans toward a New Agency to Control Who and What Enters," *New York Times*, March 20, 2001, p. A1.

31. "The Presidential Decision Directive on CI-21: Counterintelligene for the 21st Century" (The White House, Office of the Press Secretary, January 5, 2001).

32. For useful ideas, see William Wechsler, "Law in Order: Reconstructing National Security," *The National Interest*, no. 67 (Spring 2002), pp. 17–28.

33. *Quadrennial Defense Review Report* (U.S. Department of Defense, September 2001), p. 17.

34. Quoted in James Dao, "Pentagon Is Seeking New Antiterror Command," *New York Times*, February 6, 2002, p. A11.

35. Donald Rumsfeld, "Special Briefing on the Unified Command Plan" (The Pentagon, April 17, 2002). Available at http://www.defenselink.mil/news/Apr2002/t04172002_t0417sd.html (April 2002).

36. Bradley Graham and Bill Miller, "Pentagon Debates Homeland Defense Role," *Washington Post*, February 11, 2002, p. A6.

37. Hart-Rudman Commission, *Roadmap for National Security,* p. 25.

38. Erin Q. Winograd, "DoD to Establish Permanent Homeland Security Organization," *InsideDefense.com*, March 12, 2002.

39. Hart-Rudman Commission, *Roadmap for National Security,* p. 25.

Chapter 8

1. For an analysis, see Michael E. O'Hanlon, *Defense Policy Choices for the Bush Administration,* 2d ed. (Brookings, 2002).

Appendix A

1. The "reasonably foreseeable" condition is typically imposed by the courts under strict liability.

2. The Air Transportation Safety and System Stabilization Act, however, restricted air carrier liability arising from the terrorist attacks on September 11, 2001, to the limits of liability coverage maintained by the air carrier. The statute also limits air carrier liability to a total of $100 million for all claims arising as a result of an act of terrorism committed within 180 days after passage of the act.

3. In this instance, juries might now reasonably expect firms to be required to make available plastic gloves or face masks to workers who may face especially high risks of contracting anthrax from the mail, especially those in mail rooms.

4. See Peter Huber and Robert Litan, eds., *The Liability Maze: The Impact of Liability Law on Safety and Innovation* (Brookings, 1991).

CONTRIBUTORS

MICHAEL E. O'HANLON is a senior fellow in Foreign Policy Studies and holds the Sydney Stein Jr. Chair in International Security.

PETER R. ORSZAG is Joseph A. Pechman Senior Fellow in Economic Studies.

IVO H. DAALDER is a senior fellow in Foreign Policy Studies and holds the Sydney Stein Jr. Chair in International Security.

I. M. (MAC) DESTLER is professor and director of the Program on International Security and Economic Policy at the School of Public Affairs, University of Maryland.

DAVID GUNTER is a research assistant in Economic Studies.

ROBERT E. LITAN is vice president and director of Economic Studies and holds the Cabot Family Chair in Economics.

JAMES B. STEINBERG is vice president and director of Foreign Policy Studies.

INDEX